HENRI DUPARC

COMPLETE SONGS

Edited by / Herausgegeben von / Édition de

Roger Nichols

With texts in English, German and French

High Voice
Hohe Stimme
Voix élevées

EIGENTUM DES VERLEGERS · ALLE RECHTE VORBEHALTEN
ALL RIGHTS RESERVED

EDITION PETERS
LONDON · FRANKFURT/M. · LEIPZIG · NEW YORK

Cover picture: Gustave Courbet, *La Mer Orageuse* or *La Vague,* 1870
Cover design by c eye, London

© Copyright 2005 (all text, translations and music setting) by Hinrichsen Edition, Peters Edition Ltd, London

CONTENTS / INHALT / TABLE

PREFACE v
PRÉFACE vi
VORWORT viii
SONG TEXTS / LIEDTEXTE / TEXTES DES MÉLODIES xi

Page

1. Chanson triste 1
2. Soupir 6
3. Romance de Mignon 10
4. Sérénade 16
5. Le galop 20
6. Au pays où se fait la guerre 29
7. L'invitation au voyage 37
8. La vague et la cloche 46
9. La fuite 56
10. Élégie 69
11. Extase 74
12. Le manoir de Rosemonde 77
13. Sérénade florentine 81
14. Phidylé 84
15. Lamento 93
16. Testament 97
17. La vie antérieure 107

CRITICAL COMMENTARY 113

PREFACE

Editorial Method and Sources

The primary source for this volume is the edition Duparc published with Rouart, Lerolle et Cie in 1911. This edition, although often referred to as a 'nouvelle édition complète', in fact contained only 13 songs, omitting the duet *La fuite* and three early songs, *Romance de Mignon*, *Sérénade* (not to be confused with the later *Sérénade florentine*) and *Le galop*. The fact that each song retained its original plate number reflected Salabert's policy of simply combining previous printings into a typographically heterogeneous collection. The present edition is the first to present all Duparc's 17 songs in a uniform typeface.

As recorded in the Critical Commentary to each song, autograph manuscripts and earlier editions have been consulted where available. Regrettably, it has not been possible to trace eight manuscripts used for engraving, which passed through a Paris auction house in 1991 and are now in the USA. The policy throughout has been to try and ascertain Duparc's latest thoughts on the music text (*Fassung letzter Hand*). Therefore the main text does not include readings from before the 1911 edition, among which are Duparc's orchestrations of *Phidylé* and *L'invitation au voyage* (first performed in 1893 and 1897 respectively), with the single exception of three metronome marks for the latter. Readings given in round brackets are taken from the six orchestrations Duparc completed or revised between 1911 and 1913 (of *Chanson triste*, *Au pays où se fait la guerre*, *La vague et la cloche*, *Le manoir de Rosemonde*, *Testament* and *La vie antérieure*); also from his 1914 autograph of *L'invitation au voyage* (**A3** in the Critical Commentary). The, very few, readings given in square brackets are editorial suggestions (for instance, the *piano* marking in bar 1 of *Elégie*).

In the matter of the notation of the vocal line, I consulted many singing teachers, Heads of Vocal Studies in conservatoires, accompanists and editors of French music. The overwhelming verdict was that Duparc's essentially simple vocal lines are best served by retaining the flagged stems that he himself employed.

Acknowledgements

It is pleasant to record that, with the single exception of the eight autographs mentioned above, my researches have met with willing and often enthusiastic cooperation at every turn. I am grateful firstly to Comte Jean d'Armagnac, the composer's great-grandson, for kindly sending me copies of the autographs he holds in the family home in the Hautes-Pyrénées; to my friends and colleagues in academe - to Dr Jean-Michel Nectoux who gave invaluable advice over liaisons and pronunciation, to Professor Robert Orledge who read through the music texts and Critical Commentary and made many useful suggestions, and to Professor Rémy Stricker whose earlier researches and writings on these *mélodies* were of the greatest benefit to me; and to the distinguished bass Bernard Cottret (the son of Duparc's dentist, Roger Cottret), who has provided much useful information, including the moving letter of 1919 from Duparc to an admirer (see below). Finally, readers of the Critical Commentary will readily see how much I owe to the work of Dr Nancy van der Elst, who not only most generously lent me a copy of her thesis,[1] but sent me annotations and transcriptions she had made from autographs now unavailable or illegible, and followed the progress of this edition with unflagging enthusiasm and an eagle eye. My debt to her is greater than I can express.

Notes on individual songs

The first five songs in this volume were published together by Flaxland as *5 Mélodies op. 2* in 1869, when Duparc was 21. He retained only two of them (*Chanson triste* and *Soupir*) for his 1911 edition. Of the dedicatees, Léon Mac Swiney was Duparc's brother-in-law, Arthur Coquard was a fellow pupil of César Franck, Dr Guéneau de Mussy was a relation by marriage and Arthur Duparc was the composer's brother. From this time onwards, Duparc published all his songs initially as single items.

Au pays où se fait la guerre: this song dates from around 1869/70 and was originally intended for Duparc's opera *Roussalka*, which he ultimately abandoned.

L'invitation au voyage: this was the first of three songs Duparc composed while in the garrison defending Paris during the siege by the Prussians in the winter of 1870–71. In 1910 Duparc wrote how this song reminded him of the friends of his youth, now dead, and especially his mentor César Franck 'teaching me the little that I know'. Although the 1911 high voice edition prints the song in C minor and the medium voice one in A minor, the three extant autographs of the piano version are all in B♭ minor; in a letter to his publisher Lerolle of 26 August 1920 Duparc explained that this key is more comfortable for medium voices than A minor; but that Baudoux, the publisher of the first edition of 1894, was afraid of so many flats (in Salabert Archives). The present medium voice edition restores Duparc's original key – which also has the virtue of making some RH passages easier to stretch.

La vague et la cloche: Duparc wrote this initially for voice and orchestra. For the first edition with piano of 1894, his friend Vincent d'Indy made the piano reduction which, while very faithful to the original, is very hard to play. Duparc made his own, more playable version in the same year. He dedicated the song to d'Indy, who in turn dedicated his symphonic poem *Le camp de Wallenstein* to Duparc.

La fuite: the dedicatee, Henri Regnault, was a painter and a friend of the Duparcs, who was killed defending Paris on 19 January 1871. He had an excellent tenor voice, and Saint-Saëns called him 'the most musical of all the painters I have known'.

Elégie: the dedicatee of the first version, Edmond Vergnet, was a heroic tenor who sang the role of Samson in the Paris Opéra première of Saint-Saëns's *Samson et Dalila* in 1892. Henri de Lassus, the dedicatee of two later editions, was a lawyer by profession and also an excellent pianist and organist. The French translation of Moore's poem was made by Duparc's wife, Ellie Mac Swiney and the song dates from 1874.

Extase: the composer Pierre de Bréville claimed that 'Duparc was irritated by the way critics were using "Wagnerism" as a standard form of abuse, so he amused himself by deliberately writing this song "in the style of Tristan".'[2] The dedicatee, Camille Benoît, was a conservator at the Louvre and also a pupil of Franck and a composer. The date of composition is uncertain, but late in life Duparc gave 1874.

Le manoir de Rosemonde: the poet and dedicatee, Robert de Bonnières, was a friend of the composer and introduced him to the *St Matthew Passion*. Again the date of composition is uncertain, Duparc at different times giving both 1879 and 1882.

Sérénade florentine: in a letter of January 1883 Duparc mentions 'the little Florentine serenade I'm so fond of, because it gets away from the sad or violent atmosphere of the others'. The dedicatee, Henri Cochin, was a politician who also translated Dante and Petrarch and wrote a life of Fra Angelico – hence, no doubt, the dedication. The song is dated September 1880.

Phidylé: Duparc wrote this song in 1882 or 1883 and orchestrated it during the winter of 1891–2.

Lamento: Duparc had a predilection for this song,[3] which probably dates from 1883.

Testament: the dedicatee, Alice de Boissonnet, was the wife of Henri de Lassus, the dedicatee of *Elégie*, and had a fine contralto voice; Fauré also wrote three songs for her (*Automne*, *Les berceaux* and *Le secret*). The song probably dates from 1883.

La vie antérieure: in a letter to the singer Jeanne Raunay of 3 June 1909, Duparc wrote of '*La vie antérieure*, which is not in the strict sense a "mélodie", but rather a kind of sung poem in which I tried to translate into musical terms the ideas and wonderful lines of Baudelaire'.[3] The dedicatee, the composer Guy Ropartz, was a friend of Duparc. The song probably dates from 1884.

Invitation to the Journey...

Reynaldo Hahn thought that Duparc's songs treated their French texts with appalling disregard and complained that *Sérénade florentine* wasn't Florentine and wasn't a serenade.[4] Ravel thought they were imperfect... but works of genius.[5] We may well regret that a nervous disease put an end to Duparc's creativity from the mid-1880s until his death in 1933. But the supreme importance of the songs he did write has been summed up by the distinguished historian of French song, Frits Noske: 'Duparc's chief merit is that he is not content just to set words to music, but translates the poets' thoughts and feelings. It is in this way that he inaugurates an epoch in which the *mélodie* would become the preferred medium for the greatest French composers, and one to which they would entrust their most intimate and profound inspirations'.[6] Duparc's own estimation of his songs' worth, expressed in a letter of 1 August 1919 to an unknown admirer, is less sweeping but no less affecting: 'their sole merit, in my eyes, is that they are not exclusively cerebral, but that they come from the heart and speak to the heart.'

Roger Nichols

[1] Nancy van der Elst, *Henri Duparc: L'Homme et son Oeuvre*, Thèse pour le Doctorat ès Lettres, Paris, Sorbonne, 1972, pp. 462
[2] Pierre de Bréville, *Revue de la société des amis de la musique française*, May 1933, p. 83
[3] Rémy Stricker, *Henri Duparc et ses mélodies*, Paris Conservatoire (thesis), 1961, p. 60
[4] Reynaldo Hahn, *Notes; Journal d'un musicien*, Paris, Plon, 1933, pp.16–17
[5] Maurice Ravel, 'Les mélodies de Gabriel Fauré', *Revue musicale*, October 1922, III, 22–27; Eng. Trans. Arbie Orenstein, *A Ravel Reader*, Columbia University Press, 1990, p. 385
[6] Frits Noske, *French Song from Berlioz to Duparc*, Eng. Trans. Rita Benton, New York, Dover, 1970, p. 294 (amended)

PRÉFACE

Principes d'édition et sources

La source principale pour ce volume est l'édition publiée par Duparc chez Rouart, Lerolle et Cie en 1911. Cette édition, bien que souvent qualifiée de « nouvelle édition complète », ne comportait en réalité que treize mélodies, omettant le duo *La Fuite* et trois mélodies de jeunesse, *Romance de Mignon*, *Sérénade* (à ne pas confondre avec la *Sérénade florentine* ultérieure) et *Le Galop*. Le fait que chaque mélodie conserve son cotage original illustre la politique de Salabert, qui réunissait simplement des impressions antérieures dans un recueil de typographie hétérogène. L'édition que voici est la première à présenter les dix-sept mélodies de Duparc dans une typographie uniforme.

Comme l'indique le commentaire critique de chaque mélodie, nous avons consulté les manuscrits autographes et les éditions antérieures disponibles. Malheureusement, il n'a pas été possible de retrouver huit manuscrits utilisés pour la gravure, qui, après être passés par une salle des ventes parisienne en 1991, sont maintenant aux États-Unis. Le principe a été d'essayer de déterminer les dernières intentions de Duparc quant au texte musical (ce que les musicologues allemands appellent « Fassung letzter Hand »). Le texte principal ne comporte donc aucune leçon provenant de sources antérieures à l'édition de 1911, notamment des orchestrations que fit Duparc de *Phidylé* et de *L'Invitation au voyage* (créées en 1893 et 1897, respectivement), à l'exception de trois indications métronomiques pour la seconde. Les leçons données entre parenthèses proviennent des six orchestrations que Duparc acheva ou révisa entre 1911 et 1913 (*Chanson triste*, *Au Pays où se fait la guerre*, *La Vague et la Cloche*, *Le Manoir de Rosemonde*, *Testament* et *La Vie antérieure*) ; ainsi que de son autographe de 1914 de *L'Invitation au voyage* (**A3** dans le commentaire critique). Les quelques leçons entre crochets sont des suggestions de l'éditeur (par exemple, l'indication *piano* dans la première mesure de l'*Élégie*).

Pour la notation de la ligne vocale, j'ai consulté de nombreux professeurs de chant, de responsables de classes de chant dans les conservatoires, d'accompagnateurs et d'éditeurs de musique française. L'avis prédominant était que les hampes avec crochets que lui-même employait sont ce qui sert le mieux les lignes vocales essentiellement simples de Duparc.

Remerciements

C'est un plaisir de pouvoir dire que, à l'exception unique des huit autographes mentionnés ci-dessus, mes recherches ont suscité une coopération amicale et souvent enthousiaste à chaque instant. Je remercie tout d'abord le comte Jean d'Armagnac, arrière-petit-fils du compositeur, qui m'a aimablement envoyé des copies des autographes qu'il possède dans la maison familiale des Hautes-Pyrénées ; mes amis et collègues universitaires : Jean-Michel Nectoux qui m'a donné de précieux conseils sur les liaisons et la prononciation, Robert Orledge, qui a relu le texte musical et le commentaire critique, outre de nombreuses suggestions pertinentes, et Rémy Stricker, dont les recherches et les écrits sur ces mélodies m'ont été très profitables ; et l'éminente basse Bernard Cottret (fils du dentiste de Duparc, Roger Cottret), qui m'a communiqué beaucoup de renseignements utiles, ainsi que l'émouvante lettre de 1919 de Duparc à un admirateur (voir ci-dessous). Enfin, les lecteurs du commentaire critique verront combien je dois au travail de Nancy van der Elst, qui non seulement m'a généreusement prêté un exemplaire de sa thèse,[1] mais m'a envoyé des annotations et des transcriptions qu'elle avait faites sur des autographes aujourd'hui indisponibles ou illisibles, et qui a suivi les progrès de cette édition avec un enthousiasme inlassable. Ma dette envers elle est indicible.

Notes sur les mélodies

Les cinq premières mélodies de ce volume furent publiées par Flaxland sous le titre *5 Mélodies op. 2* en 1869, alors que Duparc avait vingt et un ans. Il ne conserva que deux d'entre elles (*Chanson triste* et *Soupir*) pour son édition de 1911. Parmi les dédicataires, Léon Mac Swiney était le beau-frère de Duparc, Arthur Coquard était un élève, comme

Duparc, de César Franck, le docteur Guéneau de Mussy était un parent par alliance et Arthur Duparc était le frère du compositeur. Duparc commença ensuite par publier séparément toutes ses mélodies.

Au Pays où se fait la guerre : cette mélodie, qui date de 1869–1870 environ, était destinée à l'origine à l'opéra *Roussalka* de Duparc, qu'il abandonna ensuite.

L'Invitation au voyage : c'est la première de trois mélodies que Duparc composa alors qu'il était sous les drapeaux pour défendre Paris assiégé par les Prussiens au cours de l'hiver de 1870–1871. En 1910, Duparc écrivit que cette mélodie lui rappelait ses amis de jeunesse, maintenant disparus, et surtout son mentor César Franck, qui lui avait enseigné « le peu que je sais ». Bien que l'édition de 1911 pour voix aiguë présente la mélodie en *ut* mineur et celle pour voix moyenne en *la* mineur, les trois autographes qui subsistent de la version avec piano sont toutes en *si* bémol mineur ; dans une lettre du 26 août 1920 à son éditeur Lerolle, Duparc expliquait que cette tonalité était plus confortable pour les voix moyennes que *la* mineur, mais que Baudoux, qui avait publié la première édition de 1894 (Archives Salabert), était effrayé par le nombre de bémols.

La Vague et la Cloche : Duparc écrivit à l'origine cette mélodie pour voix et orchestre. Pour la première édition avec piano de 1894, c'est son ami Vincent d'Indy qui fit la réduction pour piano, laquelle, tout en étant très fidèle à l'original, est extrêmement difficile à jouer. Duparc réalisa sa propre version, plus abordable, au cours de la même année. Il dédia la mélodie à d'Indy, qui à son tour dédia son poème symphonique *Le Camp de Wallenstein* à Duparc.

La Fuite : le dédicataire, Henri Regnault, peintre et ami des Duparc, fut tué en défendant Paris le 19 janvier 1871. Il avait une excellente voix de ténor, et Saint-Saëns le tenait pour « le plus musicien de tous les peintres que j'ai connus ».

Élégie : le dédicataire de la première version, Edmond Vergnet, était un ténor héroïque qui chanta le rôle de Samson lors de la création de *Samson et Dalila* de Saint-Saëns à l'Opéra de Paris en 1892. Henri de Lassus, le dédicataire des deux éditions ultérieures, était avocat de profession, mais aussi un excellent pianiste et organiste. La traduction française du poème de Moore fut réalisée par l'épouse de Duparc, Ellie Mac Swiney, et la mélodie date de 1874.

Extase : le compositeur Pierre de Bréville affirmait que, « impatienté par l'objection de wagnérisme devenue la "tarte à la crème" des critiques, Duparc s'amusa à écrire volontairement cette mélodie en "style de Tristan". »[2] Le dédicataire, Camille Benoît, était conservateur au Louvre, élève de Franck et compositeur. La date de composition est incertaine, mais Duparc donna sur le tard 1874.

Le Manoir de Rosemonde : le poète et dédicataire, Robert de Bonnières, était un ami du compositeur qui lui fit découvrir la *Passion selon saint Matthieu*. La date de composition est encore une fois incertaine, Duparc la situant à différents moments en 1879 et en 1882.

Sérénade florentine : dans une lettre de janvier 1883, Duparc évoque la « petite sérénade florentine à laquelle je tiens assez, parce qu'elle sort de la note triste ou violente des autres ». Le dédicataire, Henri Cochin, était un homme politique qui traduisit Dante et Pétrarque et écrivit une biographie de Fra Angelico – d'où, sans nul doute, la dédicace. La mélodie est datée de septembre 1880.

Phidylé : Duparc écrivit cette mélodie en 1882 ou 1883 et l'orchestra au cours de l'hiver de 1891–1892.

Lamento : Duparc avait une prédilection pour cette mélodie,[3] qui date probablement de 1883.

Testament : la dédicataire, Alice de Boissonnet, était l'épouse d'Henri de Lassus, dédicataire de l'*Élégie*, et avait une belle voix de contralto ; Fauré écrivit également trois mélodies pour elle (*Automne*, *Les Berceaux* et *Le Secret*). La mélodie date probablement de 1883.

La Vie antérieure : dans une lettre du 3 juin 1909 à la cantatrice Jeanne Raunay, Duparc lui parle de « La Vie Antérieure, qui n'est pas à proprement parler une mélodie mais plutôt une sorte de poème chanté où j'ai essayé de traduire musicalement la pensée et les admirables vers de Baudelaire. »[3] Le dédicataire, le compositeur Guy Ropartz, était un ami de Duparc. La mélodie date probablement de 1884.

Invitation au voyage…

Reynaldo Hahn estimait que les mélodies de Duparc témoignaient d'un effrayant irrespect pour les textes français et se plaignait que la *Sérénade florentine* n'était ni florentine ni une sérénade.[4] Ravel pensait qu'elles étaient imparfaites… mais des œuvres de génie.[5] On peut regretter qu'une maladie nerveuse ait mis un terme à la créativité de Duparc à partir du milieu des années 1880 jusqu'à sa mort en 1933. Mais l'importance suprême des mélodies qu'il composa a été bien résumée par l'éminent historien de la mélodie française, Frits Noske : « C'est là le principal mérite de Duparc : il ne se contente pas de faire chanter des paroles, il traduit les pensées, les sentiments des poètes. C'est ainsi qu'il inaugure l'époque où la mélodie sera un genre préféré des plus grands musiciens français, genre auquel on confiera les inspirations les plus intimes et les plus profondes. »[6] Le jugement de Duparc lui-même sur la valeur de ses mélodies, dans une lettre du 1er août 1919 à un admirateur inconnu, est moins péremptoire, mais non moins touchant : « Leur seul mérite, à mes yeux, est de n'être pas uniquement cérébrales, de venir du cœur et de s'adresser au cœur. »

Roger Nichols
Traduction : Dennis Collins

---

[1] Nancy van der Elst, *Henri Duparc: L'Homme et son Oeuvre, Thèse pour le Doctorat ès Lettres*, Paris, Sorbonne, 1972, 462 pages

[2] Pierre de Bréville, *Revue de la société des amis de la musique française*, Mai 1933, p. 83

[3] Rémy Stricker, *Henri Duparc et ses mélodies*, Paris Conservatoire (thèse), 1961, p. 60

[4] Reynaldo Hahn, *Notes; Journal d'un musicien*, Paris, Plon, 1933, p. 16–17

[5] Maurice Ravel, « Les mélodies de Gabriel Fauré », *Revue musicale*, octobre 1922, III, 22–27

[6] Frits Noske, *La Mélodie française de Berlioz à Duparc ; essai de critique historique*, Presses Universitaires de France, Paris, 1954, p. 260

VORWORT

Editionsmethodik und Quellen

Die Primärquelle für den vorliegenden Band ist die Ausgabe, die Duparc 1911 bei Rouart, Lerolle et Cie herausbrachte. Diese Edition wird zwar oft als „nouvelle édition complète" bezeichnet, doch enthielt sie in Wirklichkeit nur dreizehn Lieder; ausgelassen wurden das Duett *La fuite* sowie drei frühe Lieder, *Romance de Mignon*, *Sérénade* (nicht zu verwechseln mit der später entstandenen *Sérénade florentine*) und *Le galop*. Die Tatsache, dass sämtliche Lieder ihre ursprüngliche Druckplattennummer beibehielten, zeugte von Salaberts Gepflogenheit, einfach aus vorangegangenen Auflagen eine typographisch heterogene Sammlung zusammenzustellen. Die vorliegende Ausgabe ist die erste, die alle siebzehn Lieder Duparcs in einheitlichem Schriftbild vorlegt.

Wie im Kritischen Bericht zu den jeweiligen Liedern vermerkt ist, wurden wo immer möglich Autographen und ältere Ausgaben zu Rate gezogen. Leider war es nicht möglich, acht als Stichvorlagen benutzte Manuskripte einzusehen, die 1991 über ein Pariser Auktionshaus veräußert wurden und sich heute in den USA befinden. Wir haben uns durchweg bemüht, Duparcs Fassung letzter Hand zu Rate zu ziehen. Darum enthält der Haupttext keine Lesarten aus Editionen vor 1911, beispielsweise Duparcs Orchestrierungen von *Phidylé* und *L'invitation au voyage* (1893 bzw. 1897 uraufgeführt) – Ausnahmen bestehen lediglich in drei Metronomangaben für das zweite dieser Lieder. Abweichende Lesarten (in runden Klammern angeführt) entstammen den sechs Orchestrierungen, die Duparc zwischen 1911 und 1913 fertigstellte oder revidierte (von *Chanson triste*, *Au pays où se fait la guerre*, *La vague et la cloche*, *Le manoir de Rosemonde*, *Testament* und *La vie antérieure*), daneben dem auf 1914 datierten Autographen von *L'invitation au voyage* (**A3** im Kritischen Bericht). Bei den wenigen Lesarten in eckigen Klammern handelt es sich um Vorschläge des Herausgebers (wie z.B. bei der Angabe *piano* im ersten Takt der *Elégie*).

In Bezug auf die Notierung der Gesangslinie habe ich zahlreiche Gesangslehrer, leitende Stimmbildner an Konservatorien, Klavierbegleiter und Herausgeber französischer Musik konsultiert. Sie waren mehrheitlich der Meinung, dass Duparcs im Grunde schlichten Gesangslinien am besten damit gedient ist, die von ihm selbst verwendeten Notenhälse mit Fähnchen beizubehalten.

Danksagung

Es ist mir eine Freude, mitteilen zu können, dass meine Nachforschungen, mit Ausnahme der acht oben genannten Autographen, stets bereitwilliger und oft enthusiastischer Kooperationsbereitschaft begegneten. Zuvörderst möchte ich dem dem Enkel des Komponisten, Comte Jean d'Armagnac, dafür danken, dass er mir freundlicherweise Kopien der Autographen zugeschickt hat, die er auf dem Familiensitz in den Hautes-Pyrénées aufbewahrt; mein Dank gilt weiterhin meinen Freunden und Kollegen im akademischen Bereich – Dr. Jean-Michel Nectoux, der außerordentlich wertvolle Hinweise in Bezug auf Liaisons und Aussprache zu geben wusste, Professor Robert Orledge, der die Musiktexte und den Kritischen Bericht gegengelesen hat und viele nützliche Vorschläge machte, sowie Professor Rémy Stricker, dessen vorangegangene Forschungen und Schriften zu diesen *mélodies* mir von größtem Nutzen waren; des weiteren danke ich dem namhaften Bassisten Bernard Cottret, dem Sohn von Duparcs Zahnarzt Roger Cottret, der eine Menge nützlicher Information zur Verfügung stellte, darunter der bewegende Brief aus dem Jahre 1919 von Duparc an einen Bewunderer (siehe unten). Und schließlich werden Leser des Kritischen Berichts ohne weiteres erkennen, wieviel ich den Arbeiten von Dr. Nancy van der Elst verdanke, die mir nicht nur großzügigerweise ein Exemplar ihrer Dissertation geliehen hat,[1] sondern auch Anmerkungen und Transkriptionen zu seither nicht mehr zugänglichen oder unleserlichen Autographen beifügte und den Fortgang dieser Edition mit unermüdlichem Enthusiasmus und wachsamem Blick verfolgte. Ich schulde ihr mehr, als ich ausdrücken kann.

Anmerkungen zu einzelnen Liedern

Die ersten fünf Lieder des vorliegenden Bandes wurden 1869, als Duparc einundzwanzig Jahre alt war, von Flaxland zusammen als *5 Mélodies op. 2* herausgegeben. Er behielt nur zwei davon (*Chanson triste* und *Soupir*) für die Ausgabe von 1911 bei. Von den Widmungsträgern war Léon Mac Swiney Duparcs Schwager, Arthur Coquard ein Mitstudent bei César Franck; Dr Guéneau de Mussy war mit Duparc verschwägert und Arthur Duparc der Bruder des Komponisten. Von nun an brachte Duparc alle seine Lieder zuerst in Einzelausgaben heraus.

Au pays où se fait la guerre: Dieses Lied stammt aus der Zeit um 1869/70 und war ursprünglich für Duparcs Oper *Roussalka* vorgesehen, die er schließlich verwarf.

L'invitation au voyage: Dies ist das erste von drei Liedern, die Duparc komponierte, als er während der preußischen Belagerung von Paris im Winter 1870/71 zur Verteidigung der Stadt garnisoniert war. 1910 schrieb Duparc, das Lied erinnere ihn an die seither verstorbenen Freunde aus seiner Jugend, und insbesondere daran, wie sein Mentor César Franck ihm „das wenige, das ich heute weiß" beibrachte. Obwohl die Ausgabe von 1911 für hohe Stimmlage das Lied in c-Moll setzt, diejenige für mittlere Stimmlage in a-Moll, stehen die drei erhaltenen Autographen alle in b-Moll; in einem Brief an seinen Verleger Lerolle vom 26. August 1920 erläuterte Duparc, diese Tonart liege für die mittleren Stimmlagen bequemer als a-Moll, der Herausgeber der Erstausgabe von 1894 (Salabert-Archive), Baudoux, habe jedoch die vielen Erniedrigungszeichen vermeiden wollen.

La vague et la cloche: Duparc schrieb dieses Stück ursprünglich für Gesangsstimme und Orchester. Für die erste Ausgabe mit Klavierbegleitung von 1894 erstellte sein Freund Vincent d'Indy den Klavierauszug, der sich zwar eng an das Original hält, aber ausgesprochen schwer auszuführen ist. Duparc fertigte im selben Jahr seine eigene, etwas leichter zu spielende Fassung an. Er widmete das Lied d'Indy, der wiederum seine Tondichtung *Le camp de Wallenstein* Duparc zueignete.

La fuite: Der Widmungsträger Henri Regnault war ein Maler und Freund der Familie Duparc, der bei der Verteidigung von Paris am 19. Januar 1871 fiel. Er hatte eine ausgezeichnete Tenorstimme, und Saint-Saëns nannte ihn „den musikalischsten aller Maler, die ich je gekannt habe".

Elégie: Edmond Vergnet, dem die erste Fassung des Lied zugeeignet ist, war ein Heldentenor, der 1892 bei der Premiere von Saint-Saëns' *Samson et Dalila* an der Pariser Opéra die Rolle des Samson sang. Henri de Lassus, der Widmungsträger der beiden späteren Ausgaben, war Anwalt von Beruf, aber auch ein ausgezeichneter Pianist und Organist. Die französische Übersetzung von Moores englischsprachigem Gedicht erstellte Duparcs Frau Ellie Mac Swiney, und das Lied stammt von 1874.

Extase: Der Komponist Pierre de Bréville berichtet: „Duparc war irritiert über die Art, wie Kritiker den Begriff ‚Wagnerismus' als gängiges Schimpfwort benutzten, darum machte er sich einen Spaß

daraus, dieses Lied absichtlich ‚im Stil des ‚Tristan' zu komponieren."
[2] Der Widmungsträger Camille Benoît war Konservator am Louvre, daneben Komponist und Schüler von Franck. Das Kompositionsdatum ist ungewiss, aber im Alter nannte Duparc das Jahr 1874.

Le manoir de Rosemonde: Der Dichter Robert de Bonnières, dem Duparc das Lied widmete, war ein Freund des Komponisten und machte ihn mit der Matthäuspassion bekannt. Auch in diesem Fall ist das Entstehungsdatum nicht genau festzulegen – Duparc nannte verschiedentlich die Jahre 1879 und 1882.

Sérénade florentine: In einem Brief vom Januar 1883 erwähnt Duparc „die kleine florentinische Serenade, die ich so schätze, weil sie sich von der traurigen oder gewaltsamen Atmosphäre der anderen abhebt". Der Widmungsträger Henri Cochin war ein Politiker, der nebenbei Dante und Petrarca übersetzte und eine Biographie des Fra Angelico schrieb – was zweifellos die Zueignung anregte. Das Lied trägt das Datum September 1880.

Phidylé: Duparc schrieb dieses Lied 1882 oder 1883 und orchestrierte es Im Laufe des Winters 1891/92.

Lamento: Duparc hatte eine besondere Vorliebe für dieses Lied,[3] das wahrscheinlich aus dem Jahr 1883 stammt.

Testament: Die Widmungsträgerin Alice de Boissonnet war verheiratet mit Henri de Lassus, dem die *Elégie* zugeeignet ist, und mit einer schönen Altstimme gesegnet; Fauré schrieb ebenfalls drei Lieder für sie (*Automne*, *Les berceaux* und *Le secret*). Das Lied entstand wahrscheinlich 1883.

La vie antérieure: In einem Brief an die Sängerin Jeanne Raunay vom 3. Juni 1909 berichtete Duparc von „*La vie antérieure*, nicht im eigentlichen Sinne eine ‚mélodie', sondern eher eine Art gesungenes Poem, in dem ich die Ideen und wunderbaren Zeilen Baudelaires in Musik umzusetzen versuchte".[3] Das Werk ist dem Komponisten Guy Ropartz gewidmet, der mit Duparc befreundet war. Das Lied entstand wahrscheinlich 1884.

Einladung, auf Reisen zu gehen…

Reynaldo Hahn meinte, Duparcs Lieder behandelten ihre französischen Texte mit schrecklicher Missachtung, und beschwerte sich darüber, dass die *Sérénade florentine* weder florentinisch sei, noch eine Serenade.[4] Ravel behauptete, sie seien fehlerhaft… aber genial.[5] Man mag bedauern, dass ein Nervenleiden ab der Mitte der 1880er-Jahre bis zu seinem Tode 1933 der Kreativität Duparcs ein Ende setzte. Doch die unvergleichliche Bedeutung der Lieder, die er tatsächlich schrieb, hat Frits Noske, der renommierte Historiker des französischen Liedschaffens, folgendermaßen zusammengefasst: „Duparcs besonderes Verdienst ist es, dass er sich nicht damit begnügt, einen Text zu vertonen, sondern die Gedanken und Gefühle des Dichters umzusetzen weiß. Insofern leitet er eine Epoche ein, in der die *mélodie* zur bevorzugten Ausdrucksform der größten französischen Komponisten werden sollte, der sie ihre intimsten und profundesten Inspirationen anvertrauen würden."[6] Duparcs Wertschätzung seiner eigenen Lieder, die er in einem Brief vom 1. August 1919 an einen unbekannten Bewunderer zum Ausdruck brachte, ist weniger allumfassend, aber darum nicht weniger bewegend: „Ihr ganzer Verdienst ist in meinen Augen, dass sie nicht ausschließlich intellektuell sind, sondern von Herzen kommen und das Herz ansprechen."

Roger Nichols
Übersetzung Anne Steeb/Bernd Müller

---

[1] Nancy van der Elst, *Henri Duparc: L'Homme et son Oeuvre*, Thèse pour le Doctorat ès Lettres, Paris, Sorbonne, 1972, 462 S.
[2] Pierre de Bréville, *Revue de la société des amis de la musique française*, Mai 1933, S. 83
[3] Rémy Stricker, *Henri Duparc et ses mélodies*, Paris Konservatorium (theses), 1961, S. 60
[4] Reynaldo Hahn, *Notes; Journal d'un musicien*, Paris, Plon, 1933, S. 16/17
[5] Maurice Ravel, „Les mélodies de Gabriel Fauré", *Revue musicale*, Oktober 1922, III, 22–27
[6] Frits Noske, *French Song from Berlioz to Duparc*, Dover, New York 1970, S. 294

EDITOR'S NOTE

Throughout the texts that follow I have added the following markings (a liaison is the carrying-over of a consonant on to the initial vowel of the following word):

Mon‿amour	liaison	[mɔnamuːr]
diras‿une	optional liaison	[dirazyn] or [dirayn]
yeux | alors	no liaison	[jøalɔːr]
ly<u>s</u>	consonant (s) sounded	[lis]
sourci*l*s	consonant (l) not sounded	[sursi]

In one or two cases the presence or absence of a liaison will depend upon the singer's choice of where to take a breath. I have established the punctuation of texts from reputable literary sources where these were available.

Dans les textes qui suivent, j'ai ajouté les indications que voici:

Mon‿amour	liaison	[mɔnamuːr]
diras‿une	liaison facultative	[dirazyn] or [dirayn]
yeux | alors	pas de liaison	[jøalɔːr]
ly<u>s</u>	consonne (s) prononcée	[lis]
sourci*l*s	consonne (l) non prononcée	[sursi]

Dans un ou deux cas, la présence ou l'absence de liaison dépendra des respirations que le chanteur choisira de faire. J'ai établi la ponctuation des textes à partir de sources littéraires de référence lorsqu'elles étaient disponibles.

In den nachstehenden Texten habe ich durchweg folgende Kennzeichnungen vorgenommen (unter Liaison ist die Bindung eines Konsonanten mit dem Anfangsvokal des folgenden Wortes zu verstehen):

Mon‿amour	Liaison	[mɔnamuːr]
diras‿une	freiwillig Liaison	[dirazyn] or [dirayn]
yeux | alors	keine Liaison	[jøalɔːr]
ly<u>s</u>	Konsonant (s) ausgesprochen	[lis]
sourci*l*s	Konsonant (l) unausgesprochen	[sursi]

In ein oder zwei Fällen hängt das Vorkommen bzw. Nichtvorkommen einer Liaison davon ab, welche Stelle der Sänger zum Atemholen wählt. Ich habe die Interpunktion der Texte aus verläßlichen literarischen Quellen übernommen, soweit diese verfügbar waren.

SONG TEXTS / LIEDTEXTE / TEXTES DES MÉLODIES

1. Song of Sadness
Jean Lahor (1840–1909)

In your heart sleeps a ray of moonlight,
of sweet summer moonlight,
and to escape the trials of life
I shall drown myself in your brightness.

I shall forget past sorrows,
my love, when you cradle
my sad heart and my thoughts
In the loving calm of your arms!

You will take my ailing head
sometimes upon your knees,
and will recite to it a ballad,
that will seem to speak of us,

And from your eyes full of sadness,
from your eyes then shall I drink
so many kisses and loving thoughts
that perhaps I shall be cured…

2. Sigh
René-François Sully-Prudhomme
(1839–1907)

Never to see or hear her,
never to call her name aloud,
but, faithfully, always to be waiting for her,
always to love her.

To open my arms and, tired of waiting,
to embrace empty air,
yet still, always to be holding them out for her,
always to love her.

Ah! To be compelled to hold them out for her
and to exhaust myself with tears,
yet to be shedding these tears unceasingly,
always to love her…

Never to see or hear her,
never to call her name aloud,
yet with an ever more tender love
always to love her.

3. Mignon's Romance
Victor Wilder (1835–1892)

Do you know it, that radiant land
where golden fruit shines in the branches?
A gentle breeze lulls the air
and the laurel is entwined with the green myrtle.
Do you know it, do you know it?
To that distant land, my beloved,

1. Chanson triste
Jean Lahor (1840–1909)

Dans ton cœur dort un clair de lune,
Un doux clair de lune d'été,
Et pour fuir la vie importune
Je me noierai dans ta clarté.

J'oublierai les douleurs passées,
Mon amour, quand tu berceras
Mon triste cœur et mes pensées
Dans le calme aimant de tes bras !

Tu prendras ma tête malade
Oh ! quelquefois sur tes genoux,
Et lui diras une ballade,
Qui semblera parler de nous,

Et dans tes yeux pleins de tristesses,
Dans tes yeux | alors je boirai
Tant de baisers | et de tendresses
Que peut-être je guérirai…

2. Soupir
René-François Sully-Prudhomme
(1839–1907)

Ne jamais la voir ni l'entendre,
Ne jamais tout | haut la nommer,
Mais, fidèle, toujours l'attendre,
Toujours l'aimer.

Ouvrir les bras, et, las d'attendre,
Sur le néant les refermer,
Mais encor, toujours les lui tendre,
Toujours l'aimer.

Ah ! ne pouvoir que les lui tendre,
Et dans les pleurs se consumer,
Mais ces pleurs, toujours les répandre,
Toujours l'aimer…

Ne jamais la voir ni l'entendre,
Ne jamais tout | haut la nommer,
Mais d'un amour toujours plus tendre
Toujours l'aimer.

3. Romance de Mignon
Victor Wilder (1835–1892)

Le connais-tu, ce radieux pays
Où brille dans les branches l'or des fruits ?
Un doux zéphyr embaume l'air
Et le laurier s'unit | au myrte vert.

Le connais-tu, le connais-tu ?
Là-bas, là-bas, mon bien-aimé,

1. Ein trauriges Lied
Jean Lahor (1840–1909)

In deinem Herzen schlummert ein Strahl
Mondlicht, lieblich sommerliches Mondlicht,
und ich will mich, um zu entfliehen diesem
mühevollen Leben, in deinem Leuchten
ertränken.

Vergessen werd ich vergangene Leiden,
mein Liebling, wenn du wiegst mein
trauriges Herz und meine Gedanken in der
liebevollen Stille deiner Arme!

Du wirst legen mein krankes Haupt,
ach, manchmal auf deine Knie
und ihm eine Ballade vortragen,
die von uns zu erzählen scheint,

und aus deinen kummervollen Augen,
aus deinen Augen werde ich trinken
so viele Küsse und Zärtlichkeiten,
dass ich davon vielleicht werde geheilt …

2. Seufzer
René-François Sully-Prudhomme
(1839–1907)

Nie mehr sie zu sehen oder zu hören,
nie ihren Namen auszurufen,
sondern immer treu ihrer zu harren,
sie immer zu lieben.

Auszubreiten die Arme und des Wartens
müde das Nichts zu umfangen,
sie aber doch immer nach ihr auszustrecken,
sie immer zu lieben.

Ach, nicht anders können, als sie nach ihr
auszustrecken,
und mich in Tränen zu erschöpfen,
aber dennoch unaufhörlich zu vergießen,
sie immer zu lieben...

Nie mehr sie zu sehen oder zu hören,
nie mehr ihren Namen auszurufen,
sondern mit einer Liebe, die immer zärtlich ist,
sie immer zu lieben.

3. Mignons Romanze
Victor Wilder (1835–1892)

Kennst du es, das strahlende Land,
wo an den Ästen goldene Früchte leuchten?
Ein sachter Wind erfüllt mit Duft die
Lüfte und Lorbeer sich vereint mit grüner
Myrte.
Kennst du es, kennst du es?
Dorthin, dorthin, Geliebter,

let us hasten our steps, to that distant land!	Courons porter nos pas, Là-bas, là-bas !	wollen wir eilig unsre Schritte lenken, dorthin, dorthin!
Do you know it, that wonderful place where everything still speaks to me of our love? Where every object says to me in sorrow: 'Who has stolen from you your joy and your happiness?' Do you know it, do you know it? To that distant land, my beloved, let us hasten our steps, to that distant land!	Le connais-tu, ce merveilleux séjour Où tout me parle encor de notre amour ? Où chaque objet me dit avec douleur : « Qui t'a ravi ta joie et ton bonheur ? » Le connais-tu, le connais-tu ? Là-bas, là-bas, mon bien-aimé, Courons porter nos pas, Là-bas, là-bas !	Kennst du ihn, den wundersamen Ort, wo alles noch zu mir von unsrer Liebe spricht? Wo jedes Ding voll Kummer zu mir sagt: „Wer hat dir deine Freude und dein Glück geraubt?" Kennst du es, kennst du es? Dorthin, dorthin, Geliebter, wollen wir eilig unsre Schritte lenken, dorthin, dorthin!

4. Serenade
Gabriel Marc (1840–1901)

If I were, my love,
the breeze with scented breath,
to caress your smiling mouth I should come,
shy and bewitched.

If I were the flying bee
or the attractive butterfly,
you would not see me casually
leave you for another flower.

If I were the charming rose
placed by a hand upon your heart,
if [I were] near your trembling presence,
I should faint with happiness.

But in vain I try to please you,
however much I groan and sigh.
I am a man, and what can I do?
Love you... Tell you so... And weep!

4. Sérénade
Gabriel Marc (1840–1901)

Si j'étais, ô mon amoureuse,
La brise au souffle parfumé,
Pour frôler ta bouche rieuse,
Je viendrais craintif et charmé.

Si j'étais l'abeille qui vole,
Ou le papillon séducteur,
Tu ne me verrais pas, frivole,
Te quitter pour une autre fleur.

Si j'étais la rose charmante
Que la main place sur ton cœur,
Si près de toi toute tremblante,
Je me fanerais de bonheur.

Mais en vain je cherche à te plaire,
J'ai beau gémir et soupirer.
Je suis homme, et que puis-je faire ?
T'aimer... Te le dire... Et pleurer !

4. Serenade
Gabriel Marc (1840–1901)

Wäre ich, o meine Geliebte,
die Brise mit dem duftenden Atem, käme ich,
deinen lächelnden Mund zu umstreichen,
scheu und verzaubert.

Wäre ich die fliegende Biene oder der
verführerische Schmetterling,
sähest du mich nicht leichtfertig einer
anderen Blume wegen dich verlassen.

Wäre ich die liebliche Rose,
die dir die Hand hat aufs Herz gelegt,
wäre ich in deiner bebenden Nähe,
würd ich vor Wonne vergehen.

Doch vergebens such ich dir zu gefallen,
wiewohl ich auch stöhne und seufze.
Ich bin ein Mann, und was bleibt mir zu
tun? Dich zu lieben... Es dir zu sagen... Und
zu weinen!

5. The Gallop
Sully-Prudhomme

Fine steed, set your mane flowing,
let the air around us be filled with voices,
let me hear the gravel of the river beds and
the undergrowth of the woods crunching
beneath your noisy hooves;

Blend your warm breath with the steam
pouring off your flanks,
with the flashing of your feet, your foam and
your blood!
Gallop as one sees an eagle, gliding over the
plain,
whip the grass into motion with the sound
of its rushing wings!

'Come on, young warriors, through the
stream, through the stream!'
Shouts the old chieftain to his horsemen,

and the sons of the desert scent pillage,
and the horses are drunk with their draughts
of fresh air.

5. Le galop
Sully-Prudhomme

Agite, bon cheval, ta crinière fuyante,
Que l'air autour de nous se remplisse de voix,
Que j'entende craquer sous ta corne bruyante
Le gravier des ruisseaux | et les débris des
bois ;

Aux vapeurs de tes flancs mêle ta
chaude haleine,
Aux éclairs de tes pieds, ton écume et
ton sang !
Cours comme on voit | un aigle,
en effleurant la plaine,
Fouetter l'herbe d'un vol sonore et
frémissant !

« Allons ! Les jeunes gens, | à la nage,
à la nage ! »
Crie à ses cavaliers le vieux chef de tribu,

Et les fils du désert respirent le pillage,
Et les chevaux sont fous du grand* air
qu'ils ont bu.

5. Der Galopp
Sully-Prudhomme

Schüttle, edles Ross, deine wallende Mäne,
auf dass die Luft um uns mit Stimmen
sich fülle, auf dass ich höre unter deinem
stampfenden Huf den Kies des Flussbetts
und das Unterholz der Wälder;

Mit dem Dampfen deiner Flanken vermenge
deinen warmen Atem,
mit dem Blitzen deiner Hufe dein Schäumen
und dein Blut!
Eile dahin, wie man den Adler übers
Flachland gleiten sieht,
wie er mit hörbarem Flügelschlag die Gräser
peitscht!

„Auf, junges Volk, ins Wasser, ins
Wasser!"
ruft der alte Stammeshäuptling seinen
Reitern zu,
und die Söhne der Wüste wittern Beute
und die Rösser sind wie trunken von der
frischen Luft, die sie geatmet.

Swim thus in space, my swift steed,
drench me with pure air, bathe me in the
wind!
The stirrup presses on your stomach, and I
have let the bridle loose;
my body is scarcely touching you, it flies in
your wake...

Smash everything, bushes, barriers,
branches;

Torrents, ditches, embankments, clear them
all with a single bound!
Gallop! I am dreaming and, eyes closed, I
cling to you;
carry me into the depths of the unknown!

Nage ainsi dans l'espace, ô mon cheval rapide,
Abreuve-moi d'air pur, baigne-moi dans le
vent !
L'étrier bat ton ventre, et j'ai lâché la bride ;

Mon corps te touche à peine, il vole en te
suivant...

Brise tout, le buisson, la barrière ou la branche ;

Torrents, fossés, talus, franchis tout d'un seul
bond !
Cours ! Je rêve, et sur toi, les yeux clos, je
me penche ;
Emporte, emporte-moi dans l'inconnu
profond !

this 'd' pronounced 't'

Drum schwimme im Äther, o mein flinkes
Ross, tränke mich mit reiner Luft, bade
mich in Wind!
Der Steigbügel schlägt dir gegen die Flanke
und ich hab die Zügel gelockert;
mein Leib berührt dich kaum, er fliegt in
deinem Gefolge dahin...

Zertrample alles, das Buschwerk, die Hürde,
den Ast;
über Sturzbäche, Gräben, Uferdämme setze
hinweg mit einem einzigen Sprung!
Eile! Ich träume und mit geschlossenen
Augen klammere ich mich fest an dir;
trage, trage mich in des Unbekannten
Tiefen!

6. To the Land where War is being Waged
Théophile Gautier (1811–1872)

To the land where war is being waged my
lover has gone;
it seems to my desolate heart that I am left
alone on earth.
As he left with a parting kiss,
he took my soul out of my mouth...

What is keeping him so long, dear God?
There is the sun setting,
and I, all alone in my tower,
I still await his return.

Pigeons are cooing on the rooftop,
cooing amorously,
a sad and charming sound;
the water flows under the tall willows.
I sense that I am close to tears,
my heart like an open lily overflows,
and I no longer dare hope.
Here is the white moon shining,
and I, all alone in my tower,
I still await his return...

Someone is striding up the stairs...

Is it he, my dearest lover?...
It is not he, but only my little page with my
lamp...
Evening winds, fly and tell him that he is
my thought and my dream,
all my joy and my heartache!
Here is the dawn breaking,
and I, all alone in my tower,
I still await his return.

6. Au pays où se fait la guerre
Théophile Gautier (1811–1872)

Au pays | où se fait la guerre
Mon bel ami s'en est allé ;
Il semble à mon coeur désolé
Qu'il ne reste que moi sur terre.
En partant | au baiser d'adieu,
Il m'a pris mon âme à ma bouche...

Qui le tient si longtemps, mon Dieu ?
Voilà le soleil qui se couche,
Et moi toute seule en ma tour,
J'attends encore son retour.

Les pigeons sur le toit roucoulent,
Roucoulent amoureusement,
Avec un son triste et charmant ;
Les eaux sous les grands saules coulent.
Je me sens tout près de pleurer,
Mon cœur comme un lys plein s'épanche,
Et je n'ose plus espérer.
Voici briller la lune blanche,
Et moi toute seule en ma tour,
J'attends encore son retour...

Quelqu'un monte à grands pas la rampe...

Serait-ce lui, mon doux* amant ?...
Ce n'est pas lui, mais seulement
Mon petit page avec ma lampe...
Vents du soir, volez, dites-lui
Qu'il est ma pensée et mon rêve,
Toute ma joie et mon ennui !
Voici que l'aurore se lève,
Et moi toute seule en ma tour,
J'attends encore son retour.

this 'x' pronounced 'z'

6. In das Land, wo man Krieg führt
Théophile Gautier (1811–1872)

In das Land, wo man Krieg führt, ist mein
Geliebter gegangen;
meinem untröstlichen Herzen scheint, es sei
außer mir niemand verblieben auf Erden.
Bei seinem Aufbruch hat er mit einem
Abschiedskuss meinem Mund meine Seele
entrissen...
Was hält ihn so lange fern, mein Gott?
Siehe, dort geht unter die Sonne,
und ich ganz allein in meinem Turm warte
noch immer auf seine Rückkehr.

Die Tauben gurren auf dem Dach,
gurren verliebt,
ein trauriger und reizvoller Laut;
das Wasser rauscht unter den hohen Weiden.
Ich spüre, dass ich den Tränen nahe bin,
mein Herz fließt über wie eine Lilie
und ich wage nicht länger zu hoffen.
Siehe, da leuchtet der bleiche Mond,
und ich ganz allein in meinem Turm warte
noch immer auf seine Rückkehr...

Da steigt jemand mit festem Tritt die
Treppe herauf...
Ist er es, mein Heißgeliebter?...
Er ist es nicht, sondern nur mein kleiner
Page mit meiner Lampe...
Abendwinde, flieget, sagt ihm, dass er mein
Gedanke ist und mein Traum,
meine ganze Freude und mein Kummer!
Siehe, da erhebt sich das Morgengrauen, und
ich ganz allein in meinem Turm warte noch
immer auf seine Rückkehr.

7. Invitation to a Journey
Charles Baudelaire (1821–1867)

My child, my sister,
dream of the sweetness
Of going far away to live together!

To love at leisure,
to love and die
in a land that resembles you!
The drowned suns
of those murky skies have,
for my spirit,
the mysterious charms
of your treacherous eyes,
glinting through their tears.

There, all is order and beauty,
luxury, calm and delight.

See on these canals
these vessels sleeping,
wanderers by nature;
it is to assuage
your slightest desire
that they come from the ends of the earth.
Setting suns
gild the fields,
the canals, the whole city,
with pink and gold;
the world falls asleep
in a warm light.

There, all is order and beauty,
luxury, calm and delight.

7. L'invitation au voyage
Charles Baudelaire (1821–1867)

Mon enfant, ma sœur,
Songe à la douceur
D'aller là-bas vivre ensemble !

Aimer à loisir,
Aimer | et mourir
Au pays qui te ressemble !
Les soleils mouillés
De ces ciels brouillés
Pour mon esprit ont les charmes
Si mystérieux
De tes traîtres yeux,
Brillant à travers leurs larmes.

Là, tout n'est qu'ordre et beauté,
Luxe, calme et volupté.

Vois sur ces canaux
Dormir ces vaisseaux
Dont l'humeur est vagabonde ;
C'est pour assouvir
Ton moindre désir
Qu'ils viennent du bout du monde.
— Les soleils couchants
Revêtent les champs,
Les canaux, la ville entière,
D'hyacinthe et d'or ;
Le monde s'endort
Dans une chaude lumière.

Là, tout n'est qu'ordre et beauté,
Luxe, calme et volupté.

7. Einladung, auf Reisen zu gehen
Charles Baudelaire (1821–1867)

Mein Kind, meine Schwester,
träume von der Wonne,
in die Ferne zu gehen, um dort zusammen zu leben!
In Ruhe zu lieben,
zu lieben und zu sterben
in einem Land, das dir gleicht!
Die feuchten Sonnen
dieses nassen Himmels
üben auf meinen Geist den gleichen
geheimnisvollen Reiz
aus wie deine trügerischen Augen,
die leuchten hinter Tränen hervor.

Dort ist alles wohlgeordnet, in Schönheit,
Frieden und Wonne.

Sieh auf den Kanälen
die von Natur
aus unsteten Schiffe schlafen;
um zu stillen
deine leise Sehnsucht,
kommen sie von überall her auf der Welt.
Die untergehenden Sonnen
kleiden die Felder,
die Kanäle, die ganze Stadt
in Rosa und Gold;
die Welt entschlummert
in warmem Licht.

Dort ist alles wohlgeordnet, in Schönheit,
Frieden und Wonne.

8. The Wave and the Bell
François Coppée (1842–1908)

Once, overwhelmed by a powerful potion,
I dreamt that amidst the waves and the noise
of the sea, I was sailing without a lantern in
the darkness, a dispirited sailor beyond hope
of reaching the shore…

The ocean spat its foam into my face
and the wind froze me with horror
to the very marrow,
the waves crashed like walls
in that slow rhythm broken by silence…

Then, everything changed… The sea and its
black chaos were stilled… Beneath my feet
the deck of the ship gave way…
and I was alone in an old belfry,

furiously astride a ringing bell.

I clung to the clanging monster desperately,
convulsively, closing my eyes with the
effort;

8. La vague et la cloche
François Coppée (1842–1908)

Une fois, terrassé par un puissant breuvage,
J'ai rêvé que parmi les vagues et le bruit
De la mer je voguais sans fanal dans la nuit,
Morne rameur, n'ayant plus l'espoir du
rivage…

L'Océan me crachait ses baves sur le front,
Et le vent me glaçait d'horreur
jusqu'aux entrailles,
Les vagues s'écroulaient | ainsi que des murailles
Avec ce rythme lent qu'un silence interrompt…

Puis, tout changea… la mer et sa noire mêlée
Sombrèrent… sous mes pieds s'effondra le
plancher
De la barque… et j'étais seul dans un vieux
clocher,
Chevauchant avec rage une cloche ébranlée.

J'étreignais la criarde opiniâtrement,
Convulsif et fermant dans l'effort mes
paupières;

8. Die Woge und die Glocke
François Coppée (1842–1908)

Einst, überwältigt von starkem Gebräu,
träumte ich, dass inmitten der Wogen und
im Rauschen des Meeres ich fuhr ohne Licht
in der Nacht, ein niedergeschlagener Ruderer
ohne Hoffnung, das Ufer zu erreichen...

Der Ozean spuckte mir seine Gischt ins
Gesicht und der Wind ließ mich vor
Entsetzen gefrieren bis ins Mark,
die Wogen stürzten in sich zusammen
wie Mauern in bedächtigem Rhythmus,
unterbrochen von Stille...

Dann änderte sich alles... das Meer und sein
schwarzes Gewühl flauten ab... unter meinen
Füßen gaben die Planken der Barke nach...
und ich war allein in einem alten
Kirchturm,
im wilden Ritt auf einer läutenden Glocke.

Ich klammerte mich verzweifelt, krampfhaft
an das klingende Monstrum, die Augen vor
Anstrengung fest geschlossen;

the tolling made the old stones tremble,
so fiercely did I continue its heavy swinging.

Why did you not say, O dream, where God is leading us?
Why did you not say whether they would not end,
the pointless labour and unending hubbub
that are the stuff of life, alas, of human life!

9. The Escape
Gautier

Kadidja: In the starless firmament
    the moon sheds its rays,
    night lends us its veil,
    away, away!

Ahmed: Do you not fear the anger
    of your proud brothers,
    the despair of your father,
    your father with his white eyebrows?

Kadidja: What to me are contempt,
    disapproval, dangers or curses?
    It is in you that my soul lives,
    away, away!

Ahmed: Courage fails me, I tremble,
    and I seem to feel the icy touch
    of their dagger
    through my breast…

Kadidja: Born in the desert,
    my steed would fly over cornfields,
    along furrows, rivalling the winds,
    away, away!

Ahmed: In the uncrossable desert,
    with no parasol to provide
    a little shade on the sand,
    no tent to give me shelter…

Kadidja: My eyelashes shall give you shade,
    and at night we shall sleep
    under the dark tent of my hair,
    away, away!

Ahmed: If the illusory mirage
    hid the true path from us,
    without food or water to drink
    we should both die tomorrow…

Kadidja: My heart bends beneath the weight
    of happiness;
    if water is not to be found at our
    stopping places,
    drink the tears of my joy,
    away, away!

Both: In the starless firmament, etc.
    My eyelashes, etc

Le grondement faisait trembler les vieilles pierres,
Tant j'activais sans fin le lourd balancement.

Pourquoi n'as-tu pas dit, ô rêve, où Dieu nous mène ?
Pourquoi n'as-tu pas dit s'ils ne finiraient pas,
L'inutile travail et l'éternel fracas
Dont est faite la vie, hélas, la vie humaine !

9. La fuite
Gautier

Kadidja : Au firmament sans étoile
    La lune éteint ses rayons,
    La nuit nous prête son voile,
    Fuyons, fuyons !

Ahmed : Ne crains-tu pas la colère
    De tes frères insolents,
    Le désespoir de ton père,
    De ton père aux sourcils blancs ?

Kadidja : Que m'importent mépris, blâme,
    Dangers, malédictions ?
    C'est en toi que vit mon âme,
    Fuyons, fuyons !

Ahmed : Le cœur me manque, je tremble,
    Et dans mon sein traversé
    De leur *kandjar** il me semble
    Sentir le contact glacé…

Kadidja : Née au désert ma cavale,
    Sur les blés, dans les sillons,
    Volerait, des vents rivale,
    Fuyons, fuyons !

Ahmed : Au désert | infranchissable,
    Sans parasol pour jeter
    Un peu d'ombre sur le sable,
    Sans tente pour m'abriter…

Kadidja : Mes cils te feront de l'ombre,
    Et la nuit nous dormirons
    Sous mes cheveux, tente sombre,
    Fuyons, fuyons !

Ahmed : Si le mirage illusoire
    Nous cachait le vrai chemin,
    Sans vivres, sans eau pour boire,
    Tous deux nous mourrions demain.

Kadidja : Sous le bonheur mon cœur ploie;
    Si l'eau manque aux stations,
    Bois les larmes de ma joie,
    Fuyons, fuyons !

Deux :   Au firmament sans étoile, etc.
    Mes cils, etc.

* '*d*' *is pronounced* [kadʒar]

---

das Läuten ließ die alten Steine erzittern,
so heftig setzte ich das schwere Schwingen fort.

Warum verrietest du nicht, o Traum, wohin Gott uns leitet?
Warum verrietest du nicht, ob sie enden würden,
die sinnlosen Mühen und der unendliche Tumult, aus denen das Leben, ach, das menschliche Leben besteht!

9. Die Flucht
Gautier

Kadidja: Am sternenlosen Firmament
    vergießt der Mond seine Strahlen,
    die Nacht leiht uns ihren Schleier,
    fort, fort!

Ahmed: Fürchtest du nicht die Wut deiner
    stolzen Brüder, die Verzweiflung
    deines Vaters, deines Vaters mit
    den schlohweißen Brauen?

Kadidja: Was sind mir Verachtung,
    Missbilligung, Gefahren oder
    Flüche? In dir lebt meine Seele auf,
    fort, fort!

Ahmed: Mich verlässt der Mut, ich zittere,
    vermeine die eisige Berührung
    ihres Dolchs in meiner Brust
    zu spüren…

Kadidja: In der Wüste geboren, flöge mein
    Ross über Kornfelder, an den
    Furchen entlang gleich dem Wind,
    fort, fort!

Ahmed: In der unüberquerbaren Wüste,
    ohne Sonnenschirm, um den Sand
    ein wenig zu beschatten, ohne Zelt,
    das mir Zuflucht böte…

Kadidja: Meine Augenwimpern werden dich
    beschatten, und des Nachts schlafen
    wir unter dem dunklen Zelt meines
    Haars, fort, fort!

Ahmed: Sollte die täuschende Luftspiegelung
    den richtigen Weg verbergen,
    stürben wir beide morgen schon
    mangels Nahrung und Wasser…

Kadidja: Mein Herz beugt sich unter der
    Last des Glücks;
    fänden wir bei der Rast kein
    Wasser,
    so trinke meine Freudentränen,
    fort, fort!

Beide: Am sternenlosen Firmament, etc.
    Meine Augenwimpern, etc.

10. Elegy
Thomas Moore (1780–1852)

Oh! Breathe not his name, let it sleep in the shade,
Where cold and unhonour'd his relics are laid;
Sad, silent, and dark, be the tears that we shed,
As the night-dew that falls on the grass o'er his head.

But the night-dew that falls, though in silence it weeps,
Shall brighten with verdure the grave where he sleeps;
And the tear that we shed, though in secret it rolls,
Shall long keep his memory green in our souls.

11. Ecstasy
Lahor

On a pale lily my heart sleeps
in a sleep as sweet as death…
Exquisite death, death scented
with the breath of the beloved…
On your pale breast my heart sleeps
in a sleep as sweet as death…

12. The Manor of Rosemonde
Robert de Bonnières (1850–1915)

With his sudden, devouring tooth
love bit me like a dog…
By following the bloodstains I left,
go, and you will be able to find my track…

Take a thoroughbred horse,
leave, and follow my arduous road,
bog or vanished path,
if the wild journey does not exhaust you!

In going where I went you will see that,
alone and wounded,
I travelled through this gloomy world,

And that I thus went off to die far,
far away, without discovering
the blue manor of Rosemonde.

10. Elégie
Thomas Moore (1780–1852),
Prose translation by Ellie Duparc (1845–1934)

Oh ! ne murmurez pas son nom ! Qu'il dorme dans l'ombre, où froide et sans honneur repose sa dépouille. Muettes, tristes, glacées, tombent nos larmes, comme la rosée de la nuit, qui sur sa tête humecte le gazon ; mais la rosée de la nuit, bien qu'elle pleure en silence, fera briller la verdure sur sa couche et nos larmes, en secret répandues, conserveront sa mémoire fraîche et verte dans nos cœurs.

11. Extase
Lahor

Sur un lys pâle mon cœur dort
D'un sommeil doux comme la mort…
Mort | exquise, mort parfumée
Du souffle de la bien-aimée…
Sur ton sein pâle mon cœur dort
D'un sommeil doux comme la mort…

12. Le manoir de Rosemonde
Robert de Bonnières (1850–1915)

De sa dent soudaine et vorace
Comme un chien l'amour m'a mordu…
En suivant mon sang répandu,
Va, tu pourras suivre ma trace…

Prends un cheval de bonne race,
Pars, et suis mon chemin | ardu,
Fondrière ou sentier perdu,
Si la course ne te harasse !

En passant par où j'ai passé,
Tu verras que, seul et blessé,
J'ai parcouru ce triste monde,

Et qu'ainsi je m'en fus mourir
Bien loin, bien loin, sans découvrir
Le bleu manoir de Rosemonde.

10. Elegie
Thomas Moore (1780–1852)

O! hauche seinen Namen nicht, lass ihn im Schatten ruhen,
wo seine Überreste kalt und ungeehrt gebettet sind;
traurig, still und düster seien die Tränen, die wir vergießen, da der Nachttau niedergeht auf das Gras über seinem Haupt.

Doch der niedergehende Nachttau, mag er auch lautlos weinen,
soll mit Grün schmücken das Grab, in dem er ruht;
und die Träne, die wir vergießen, mag sie auch im Verborgnen fallen,
soll lange noch in unsrer Seele seine Erinnerung begrünen.

11. Ekstase
Lahor

Auf einer blassen Lilie ruht mein Herz in einem Schlummer süß wie der Tod…
der exquisite Tod, erfüllt vom Duft des Atems der Geliebten…
Auf deiner blassen Brust ruht mein Herz in einem Schlummer süß wie der Tod…

12. Das Schloss der Rosemonde
Robert de Bonnières (1850–1915)

Mit ihrem unvermittelt verzehrenden Zahn biss mich die Liebe wie ein Hund…
Folgend der Blutspur, die ich hinterließ, gehe hin, dann findest du meine Fährte…

Nimm ein vollblütiges Ross, mache dich auf und folge meinem beschwerlichen Weg, über Moor oder schwindenden Pfad, wenn dich die wilde Jagd nicht erschöpft!

Indem du hingehst, wo ich ging, wirst du erkennen, dass ich allein und verwundet diese düstre Welt durchwanderte

und also dahinging, um weit, weit fort zu sterben, ohne das blaue Schloss der Rosemonde entdeckt zu haben.

13. Florentine serenade
Lahor

Star whose beauty shines
like a diamond in the night,
look towards my beloved
whose eyelids are closed,
and let the blessing of Heaven
descend upon her eyes!

She sleeps… Through the window
shine into her dear room:
on her whiteness, like a kiss,
come and settle until the dawn!
And may her thoughts, then,
dream of a rising star of love!

14. Phidylé
Charles-Marie-René Leconte de Lisle
(1818–1894)

The grass is soft to sleep on beneath the cool poplars,
on the slopes with their mossy springs which,
in the flowering meadows, rising from a thousand sources,
lose themselves under the dark thickets.

Rest, Phidylé! Midday blazes down on the leaves And invites you to sleep.
Amid the clover and the thyme, alone, in the full sunlight,
the flying bees are buzzing;

A warm scent swirls where the paths bend,
the red flower of the corn nods,
and the birds, sweeping their wings over the hill, Head for the shade of the wild roses.

Rest, Phidylé!

But when the sun, moving down its brilliant arc,
sees its heat diminish,
may your loveliest smile and your sweetest kiss Reward me for my wait!

15. Lament
Gautier

Do you know the white tomb,
over which floats the shadow of a yew-tree
with its plaintive sound?
On the yew, a pale dove,
sad and lonely in the setting sun,
sings its song.

One would say that the awakened soul
is weeping below the earth in unison
with the song,

13. Sérénade florentine
Lahor

Etoile dont la beauté luit
Comme un diamant dans la nuit,
Regarde vers ma bien-aimée
Dont la paupière s'est fermée,
Et fais descendre sur ses yeux
La bénédiction des cieux !

Elle s'endort… Par la fenêtre
En sa chambre heureuse pénètre :
Sur sa blancheur, comme un baiser,
Viens jusqu'à l'aube te poser !
Et que sa pensée, alors, rêve
D'un astre d'amour qui se lève !

14. Phidylé
Charles-Marie-René Leconte de Lisle
(1818–1894)

L'herbe est molle au sommeil sous les frais peupliers,
Aux pentes des sources moussues,
Qui dans les prés en fleur, germant par mille issues,
Se perdent sous les noirs | halliers.

Repose, ô Phidylé ! Midi sur les feuillages Rayonne et t'invite au sommeil.
Par le trèfle et le thym, seules, en plein soleil,
Chantent les abeilles volages ;

Un chaud parfum circule au détour des sentiers,
La rouge fleur des blés s'incline,
Et les oiseaux, rasant de l'aile la colline,
Cherchent l'ombre des églantiers.

Repose, ô Phidylé !

Mais, quand l'Astre, incliné sur sa courbe éclatante,
Verra ses ardeurs s'apaiser,
Que ton plus beau sourire et ton meilleur baiser
Me récompensent de l'attente !

15. Lamento
Gautier

Connaissez-vous la blanche tombe
Où flotte avec un son plaintif
L'ombre d'un if ?
Sur l'if une pâle colombe,
Triste et seule au soleil couchant,
Chante son chant.

On dirait que l'âme éveillée
Pleure sous terre à l'unisson
De la chanson,

13. Florentinische Serenade
Lahor

Stern, dessen Schönheit
diamantengleich die Nacht erhellt,
schau aus nach meiner Liebsten
mit den geschlossnen Lidern
und lass des Himmels Segen auf ihre Augen
niedergehn!

Sie schläft… Durchs Fenster
leuchte in ihre reizende Kammer:
Komm und ruhe, einem Kusse gleich,
auf ihrer Weiße bis zum Morgen!
Und mögen ihre Gedanken drum
träumen vom aufgehenden Liebesstern!

14. Phidylé
Charles-Marie-René Leconte de Lisle
(1818–1894)

Das Gras lädt weich zum Schlafe unter den kühlen Pappeln
an Hängen mit bemoosten Quellen,
die in den blühenden Wiesen aus tausend Bornen entspringen,
um sich unter dunklem Dickicht zu verlieren.

So ruhe denn, Phidylé! Der Mittag brennt aufs Laubwerk herab und lädt dich zum Schlummer.
Inmitten von Klee und Quendel allein,
im strahlenden Sonnenschein summen die fliegenden Bienen;

Ein warmer Duft wirbelt umher an der Beuge der Pfade,
die pupurne Kornblüte neigt sich,
und die Vögel breiten ihre Schwingen überm Hügel, streben in den Schatten der wildwachsenden Rosen.

So ruhe denn, Phidylé!

Doch wenn die Sonne absinkt auf ihrer strahlenden Bahn und spürt,
wie ihre Hitze nachlässt,
sollen dein lieblichstes Lächeln und dein süßester Kuss mich für meine Geduld belohnen!

15. Klage
Gautier

Kennst du das weiße Grabmal,
über dem der Schatten einer Eibe schwebt
mit Trauerklang?
In der Eibe singt eine fahle Taube
bekümmert und einsam im Licht des
Sonnenuntergangs ihr Lied.

Man meint, die erwachte Seele weine unter
der Erde im Einklang mit diesem Lied und
gurre sehr,

and coos its lament, very gently,
at the misery of being forgotten.

Ah! Nevermore shall I go near the tomb,
when night descends
with its dark cloak,
to hear the pale dove singing,
on the branch of a yew,
its plaintive song!

16. Testament
Armand Silvestre (1837–1901)

So that the wind may bring them to you
on the black wing of remorse,
I shall write on a dead leaf
the torments of my dead heart!

All my sap has been dried up
in the bright middays of your beauty,
and, like a withered leaf,
nothing of life remains in me;

Your eyes have scorched me to my soul,
like suns without pity!
Like a leaf swallowed up by the abyss,
the south wind will carry me away also…

But before then, so that it may bring them to you
on the black wing of remorse,
I shall write on a dead leaf
the torments of my dead heart!

17. Past life
Baudelaire

Long have I lived beneath vast porticoes,
touched by sea-borne suns with a thousand fires,
and whose tall pillars, upright and majestic,
of an evening made them resemble caves of basalt.

The surging waves, rolling reflection of the sky,
blended in solemn and mysterious fashion
the all-powerful chords of their rich music
with the colours of the setting sun reflected in my eyes.

It is there that I lived a life of calm delights,
amid the blue sky, waves, splendours
and naked slaves, lavishly scented,

Who cooled my forehead with palms,
and whose sole care was to deepen
the painful secret that made me languish.

Translation by Roger Nichols

Et du malheur d'être oubliée
Se plaint dans un roucoulement,
Bien doucement.

Ah ! jamais plus près de la tombe
Je n'irai, quand descend le soir
Au manteau noir,
Ecouter la pâle colombe
Chanter, sur la branche de l'if,
Son chant plaintif !

16. Testament
Armand Silvestre (1837–1901)

Pour que le vent te les apporte
Sur l'aile noire d'un remord,
J'écrirai sur la feuille morte
Les tortures de mon cœur mort !

Toute ma sève s'est tarie
Aux clairs midis de ta beauté,
Et, comme à la feuille flétrie,
Rien de vivant ne m'est resté ;

Tes yeux m'ont brûlé jusqu'à l'âme,
Comme des soleils sans merci !
Feuille que le gouffre réclame,
L'autan va m'emporter aussi…

Mais avant, pour qu'il te les porte

Sur l'aile noire d'un remord,
J'écrirai sur la feuille morte
Les tortures de mon cœur mort !

17. La vie antérieure
Baudelaire

J'ai longtemps habité sous de vastes portiques
Que les soleils marins teignaient de mille feux,
Et que leurs grands piliers, droits et majestueux,
Rendaient pareils, le soir, aux grottes basaltiques.

Les | houles, en roulant les images des cieux,
Mêlaient d'une façon solennelle et mystique
Les tout-puissants accords de leur riche musique
Aux couleurs du couchant reflété par mes yeux.

C'est là que j'ai vécu dans les voluptés calmes,
Au milieu de l'azur, des vagues, des splendeurs
Et des esclaves nus, tout imprégnés d'odeurs,

Qui me rafraîchissaient le front | avec des palmes,
Et dont l'unique soin | était d'approfondir
Le secret douloureux qui me faisait languir.

sehr sanft ihre Klage über das Elend,
dass man sie vergaß.

Ach! Niemals wieder nähere ich mich dem
Grab, wenn die Nacht alles
in Dunkel hüllt,
um zu lauschen dem klagenden Gesang
der fahlen Taube
im Geäst der Eibe!

16. Testament
Armand Silvestre (1837–1901)

Dass der Wind sie dir bringe
auf der Reue schwarzen Schwingen,
will ich schreiben auf ein totes Blatt die
Qualen meines toten Herzens!

All mein Lebenssaft ist vertrocknet im
grellen Mittagsstrahlen deiner Schönheit
und, einem welken Blatte gleich,
ist mir alles Lebendige entzogen;

Deine Augen haben sich in meine Seele
gebrannt wie gnadenlose Sonnen!
Wie ein Blatt, das der Abgrund verschlang,
trägt auch mich der Südwind davon…

Doch zuvor, dass er sie dir bringe auf der

Reue schwarzen Schwingen,
will ich schreiben auf ein totes Blatt die
Qualen meines toten Herzens!

17. Das frühere Leben
Baudelaire

Lang wohnte ich in riesenhaften Portiken,
in tausend Feuer bunt getaucht von
Meeressonnen,
und deren hohe Säulen glichen, aufrecht und
erhaben,
des Abends Grotten aus Basalt.

Brandende Wellen, wogende Spiegelung des
Himmels,
mischten feierlich und geheimnisvoll
allmächtige Akkorde ihrer volltönenden
Musik mit den in meinen Augen
reflektierten Farben der untergehenden
Sonne.

Dort war's, wo ich ein Leben stiller Wonnen
führte inmitten des azurnen Himmels, der
Wogen, aller Pracht und nackter Sklaven,
duftgetränkt,

die meine Stirn mit Palmen kühlten und
deren einzige Sorge war, noch zu vertiefen
jenes quälende Geheimnis, das mich
dahinsiechen ließ.

Übersetzung Anne Steeb/Bernd Müller

à ma mère

2. Soupir
(Sully–Prudhomme)

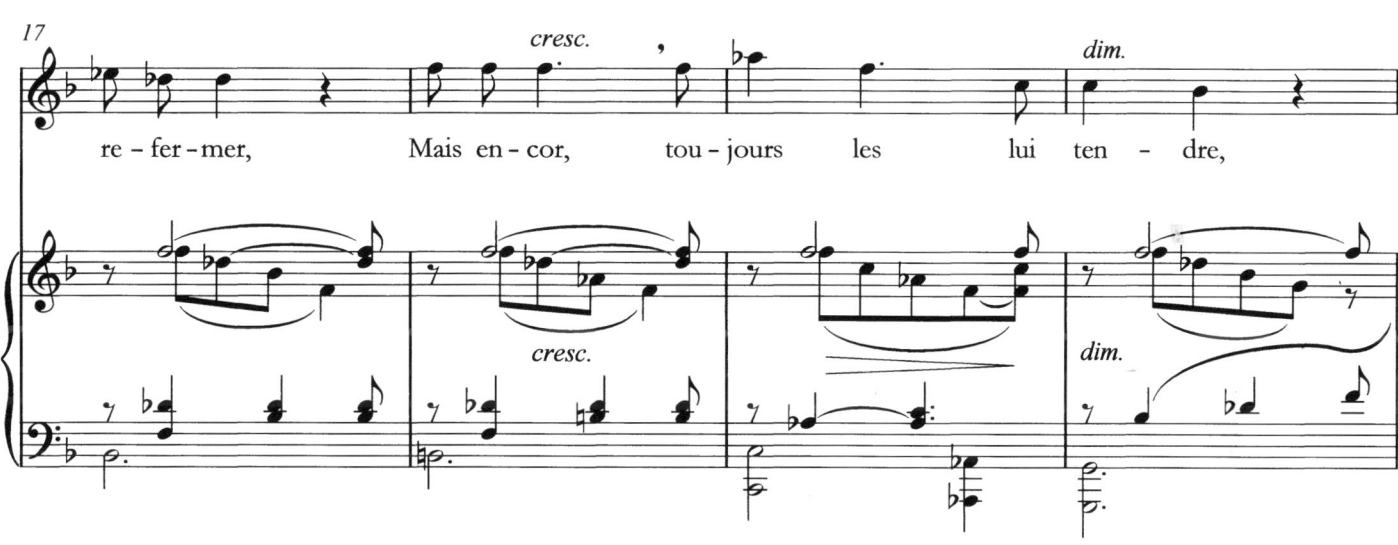

à mon ami Arthur Coquard

3. Romance de Mignon

(Wilder, after Goethe)

Le con - nais - tu, ce ra - di - eux pa - ys

Où bril - le dans les bran - ches l'or des fruits ?

Un doux zé - phir em - bau - me l'air Et

1) See Critical Commentary

à mon ami Noël Gueneau de Mussy

4. Sérénade

(Marc)

à mon frère Arthur Duparc

5. Le galop
(Sully-Prudhomme)

Allegro non troppo ma con fuoco

A - gi - te, bon che - val, ta cri - niè - re fuy - an - te, Que l'air au - tour de nous se rem - plis - se de voix, Que j'en-

à Mademoiselle Eugénie Vergin

6. Au pays où se fait la guerre
(Gautier)

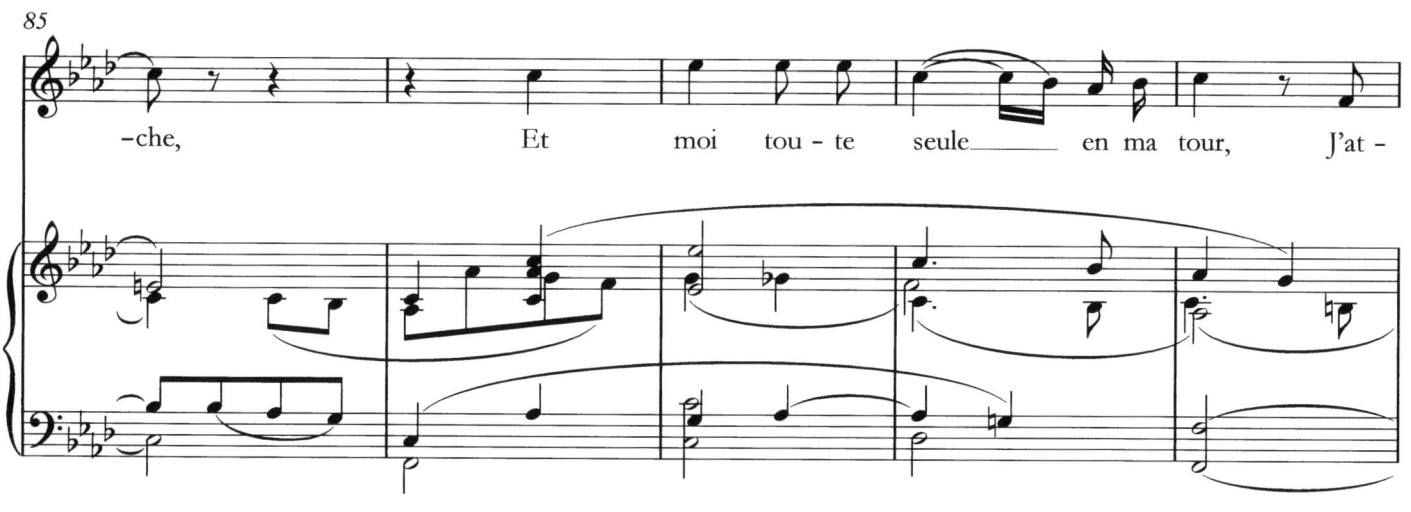
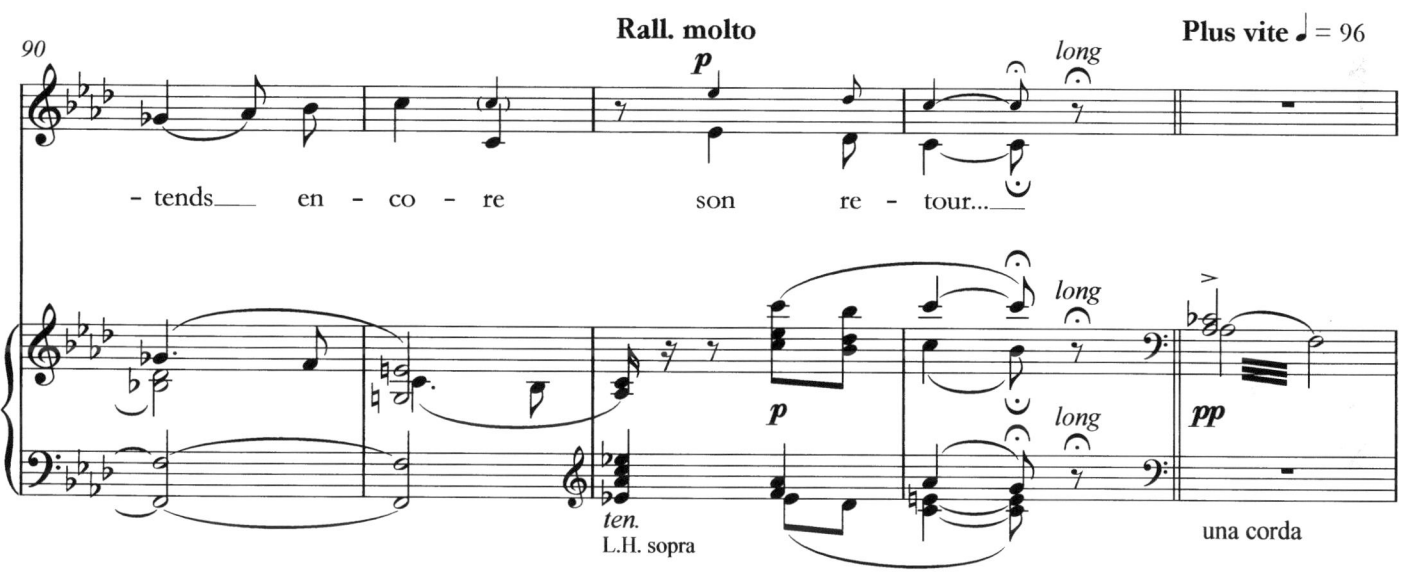
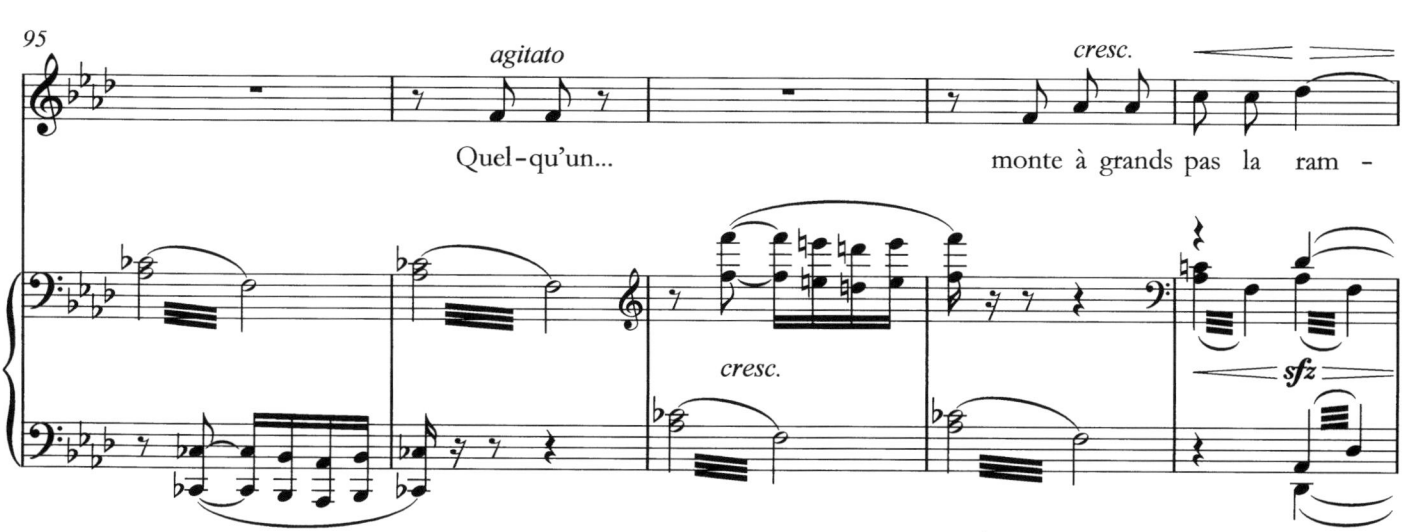

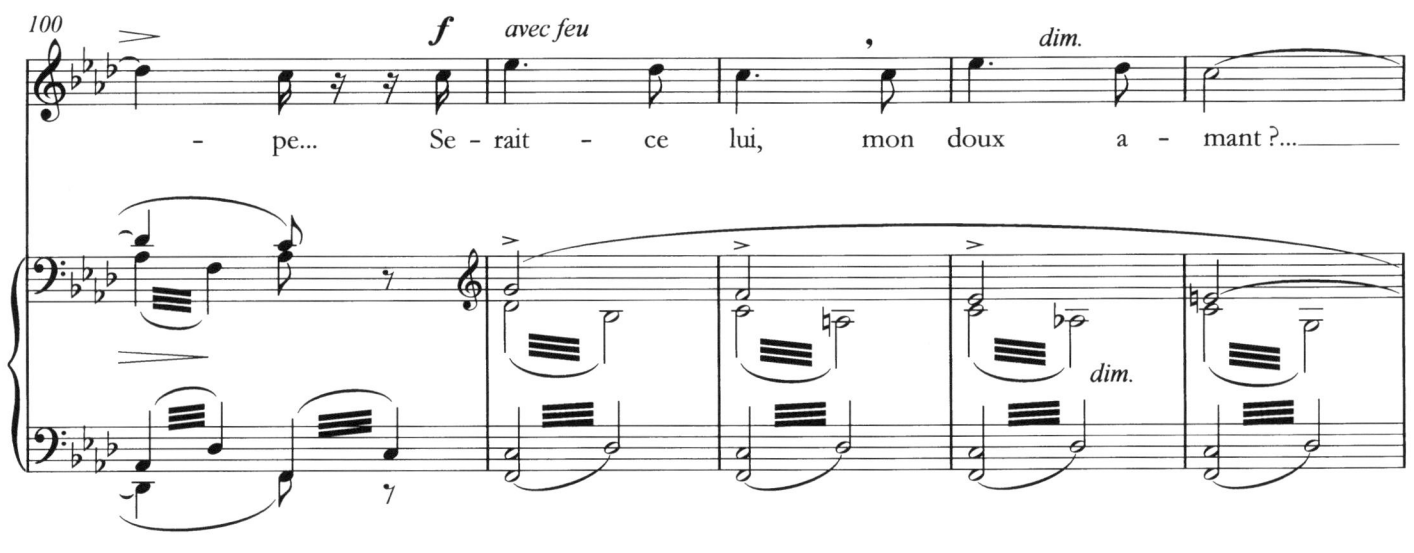
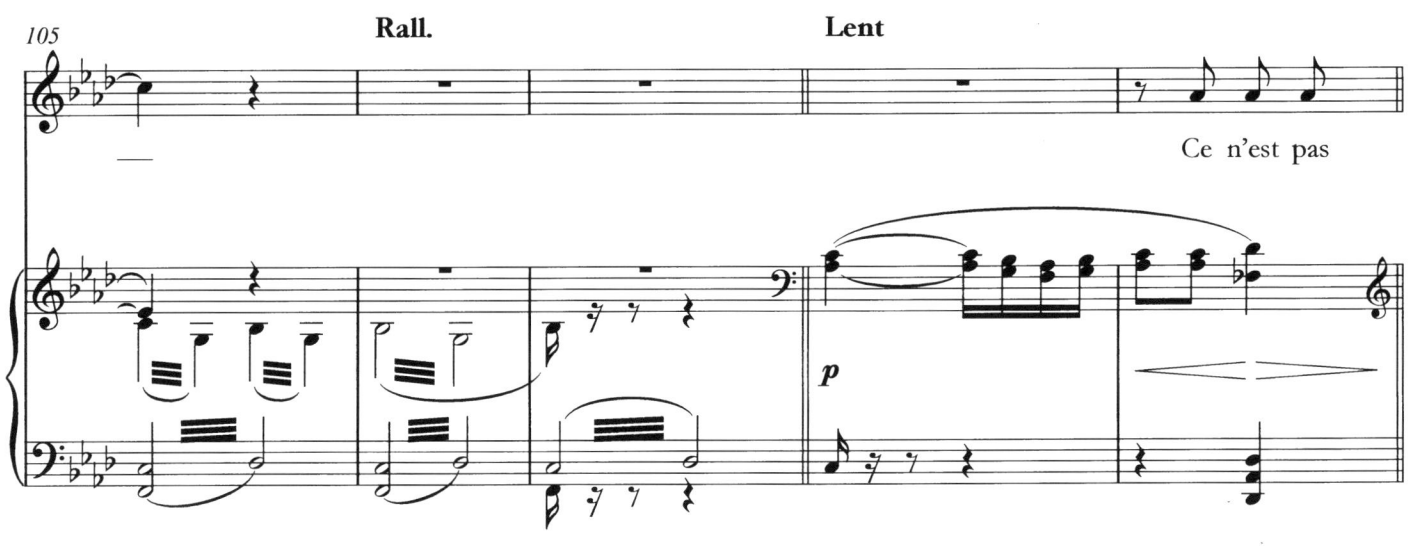

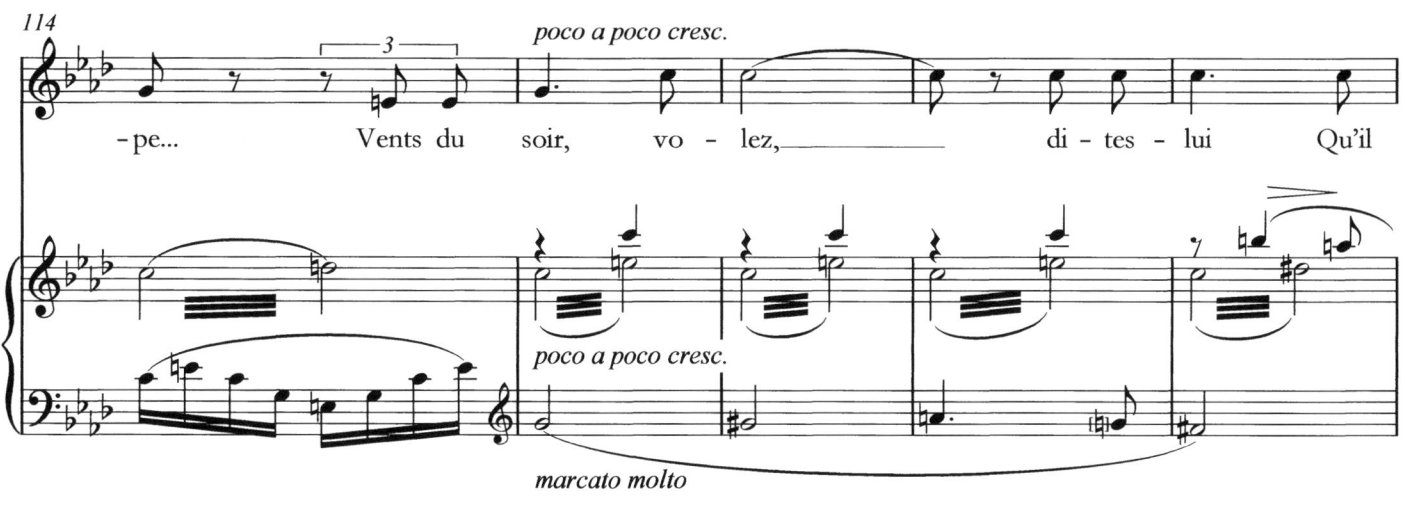
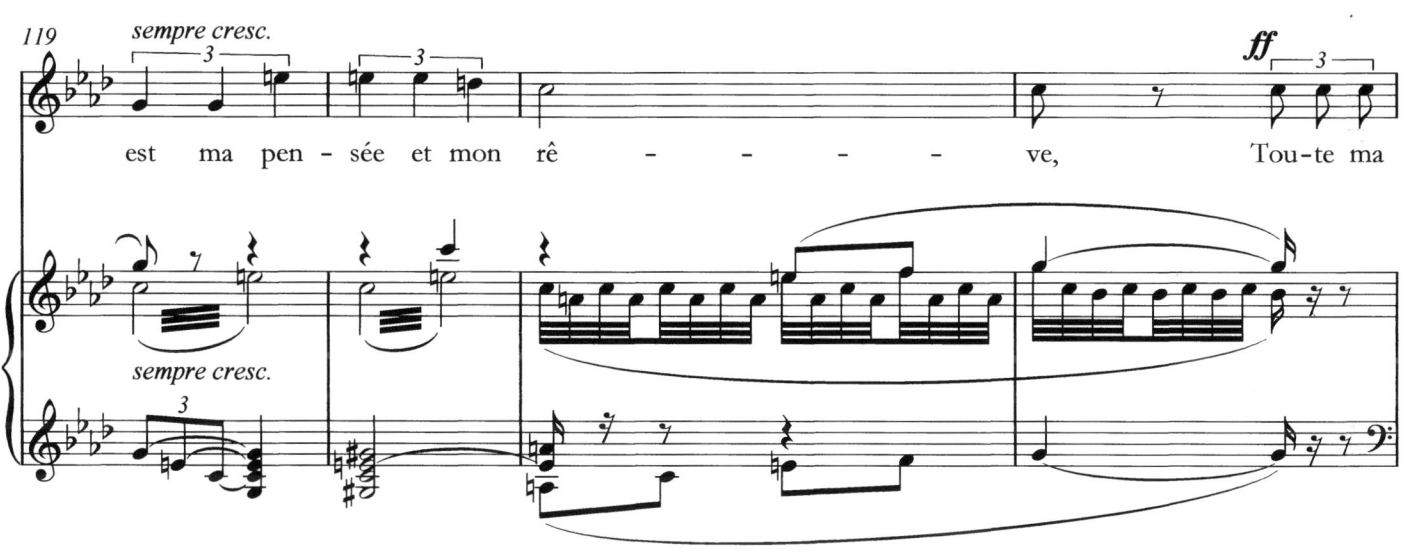

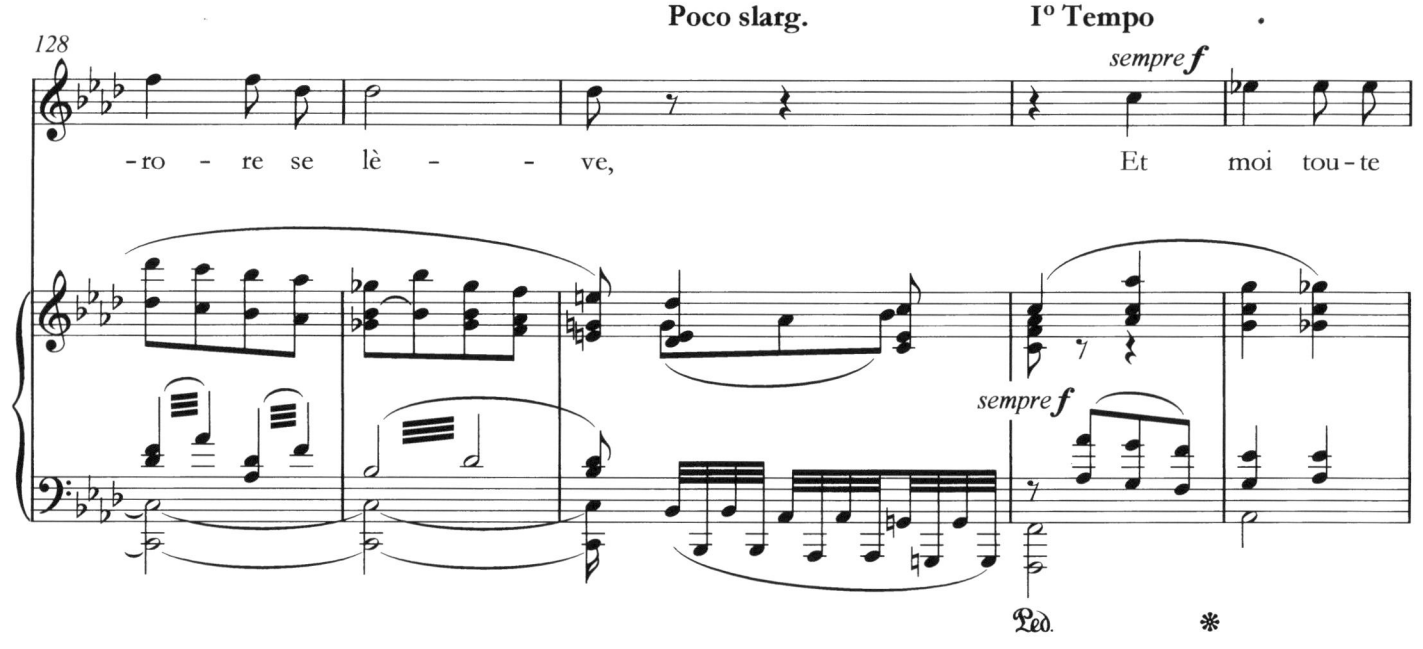

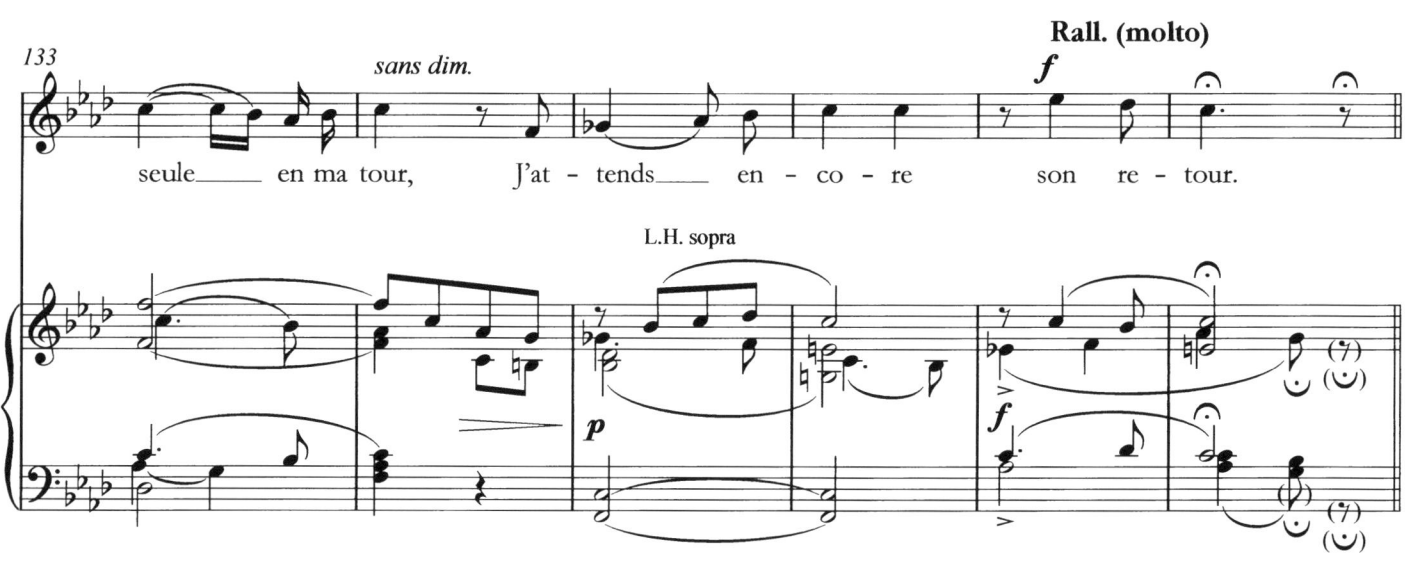

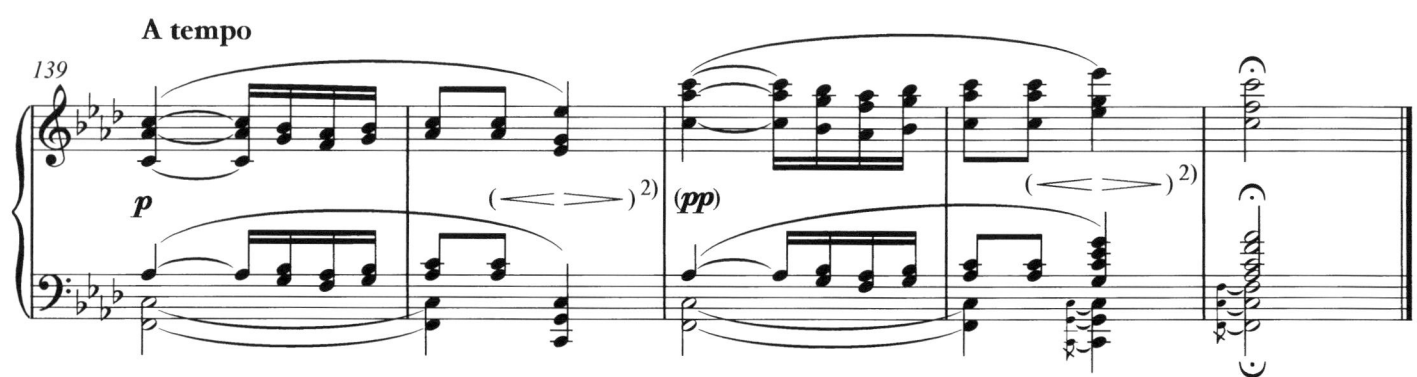

2) See Critical Commentary

à Madame Henri Duparc

7. L'invitation au voyage
(Baudelaire)

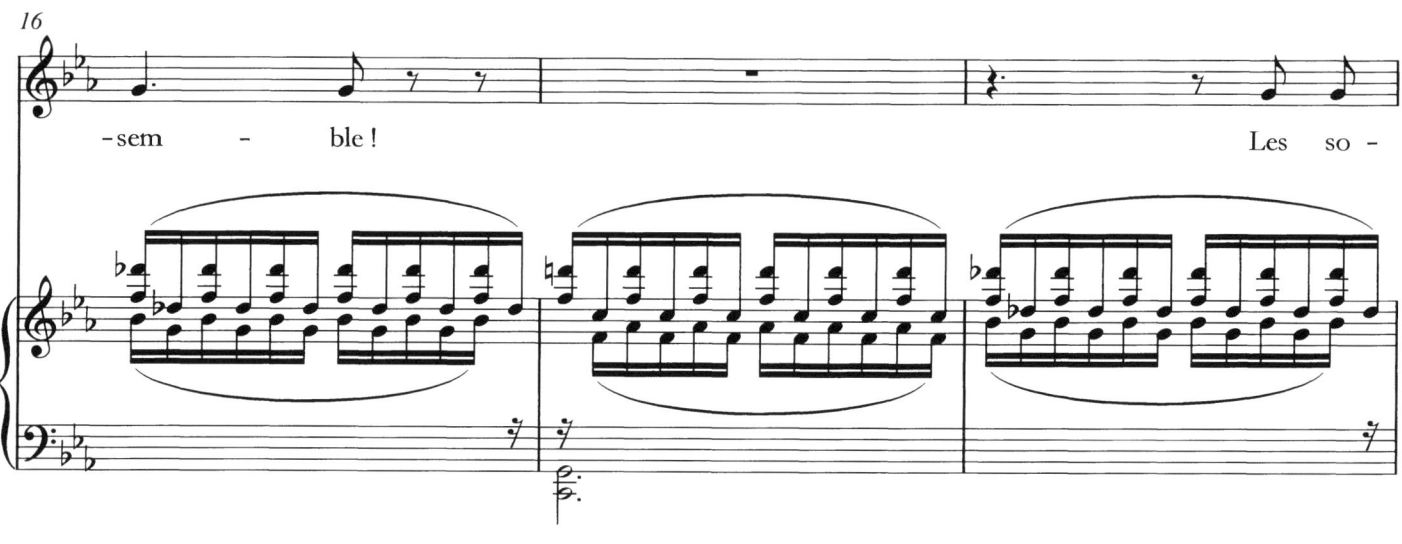
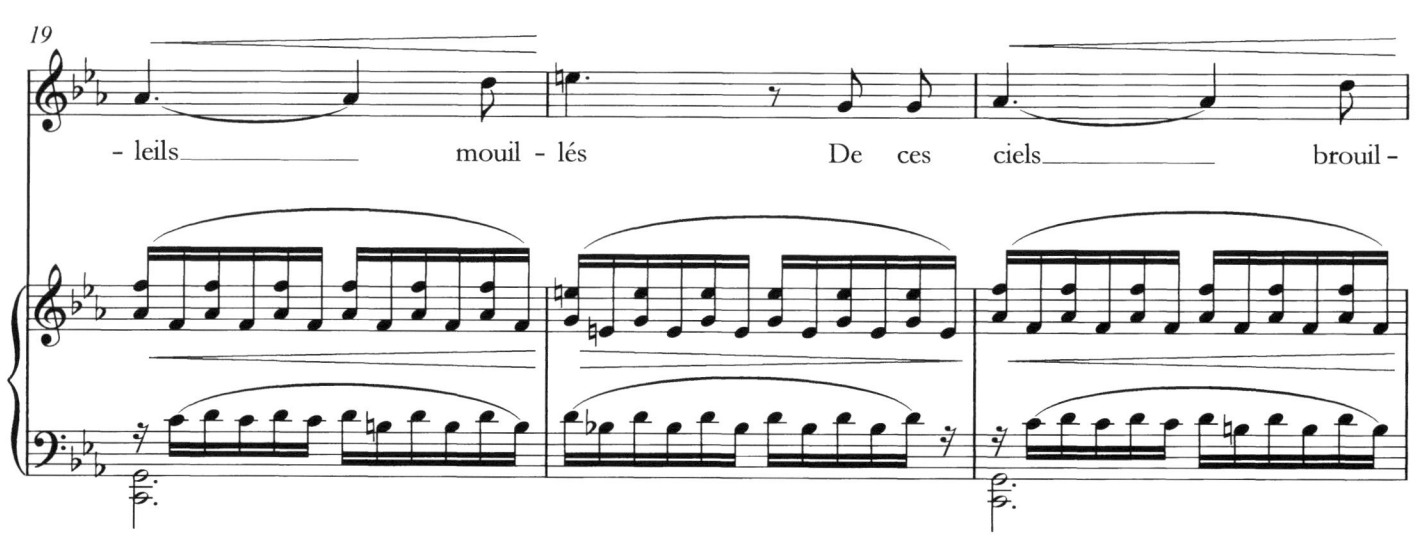

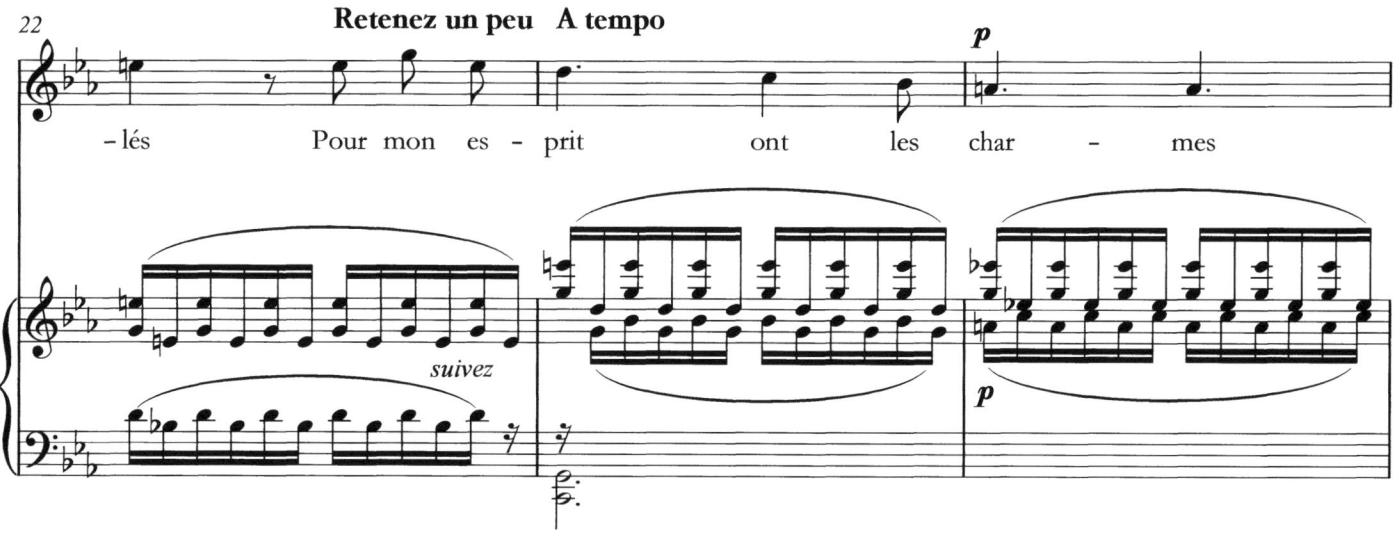
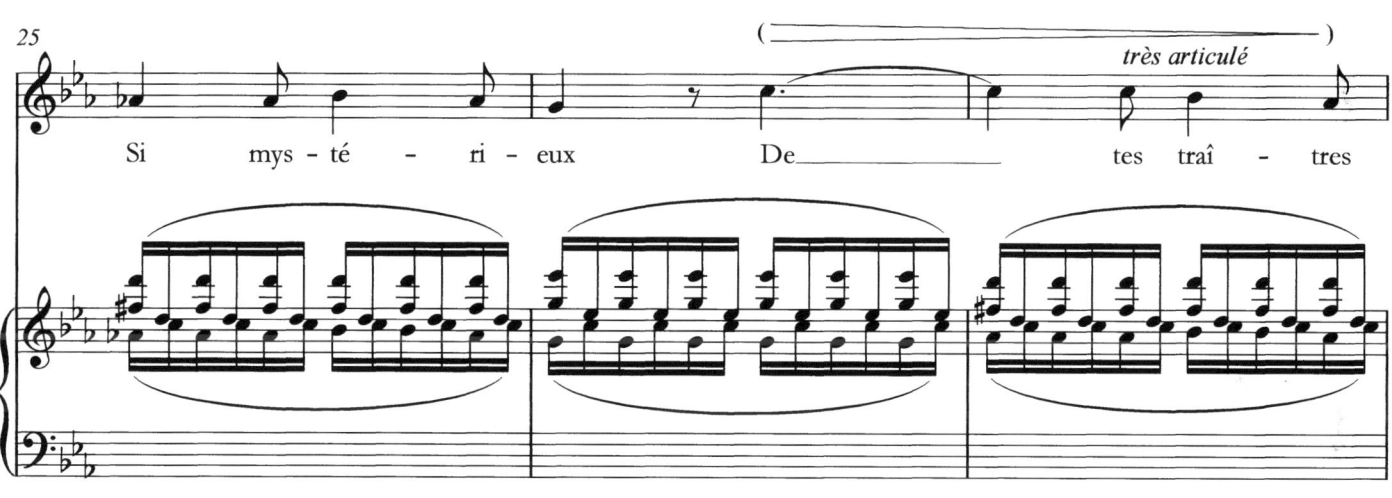
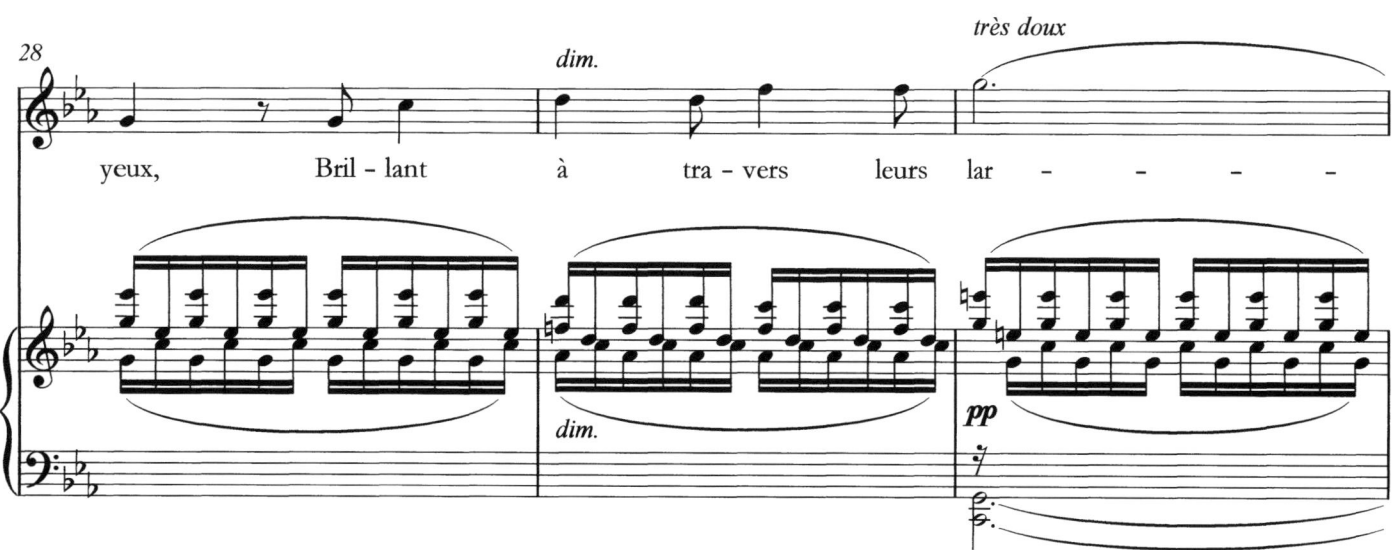

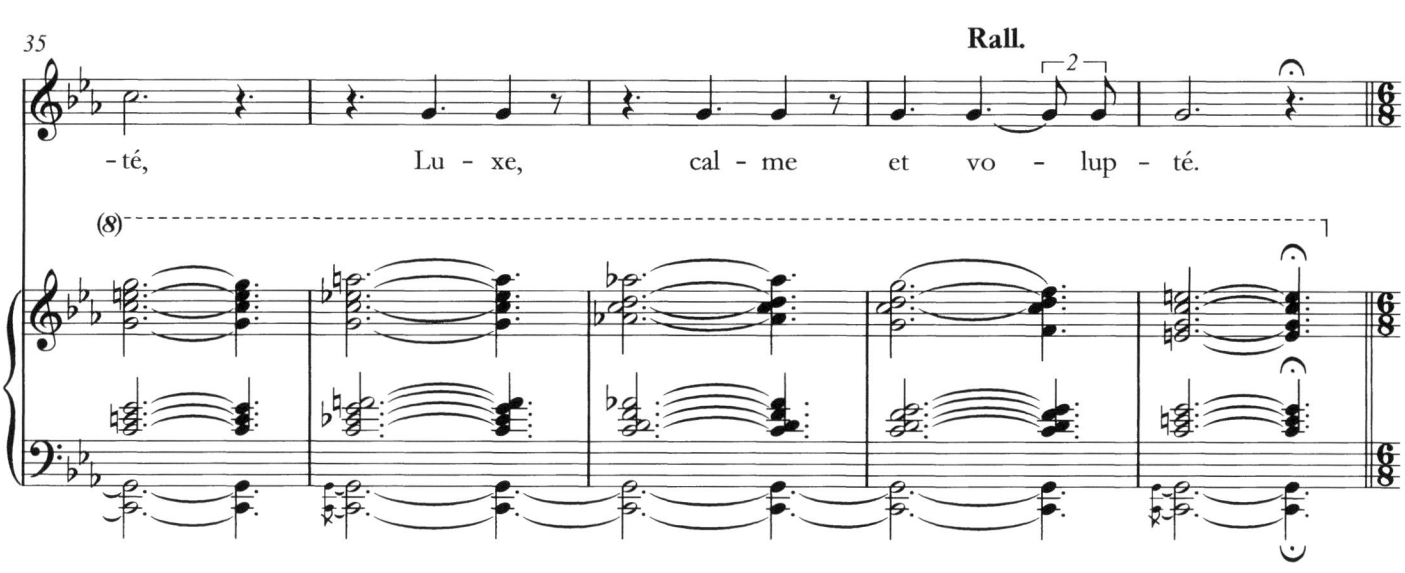
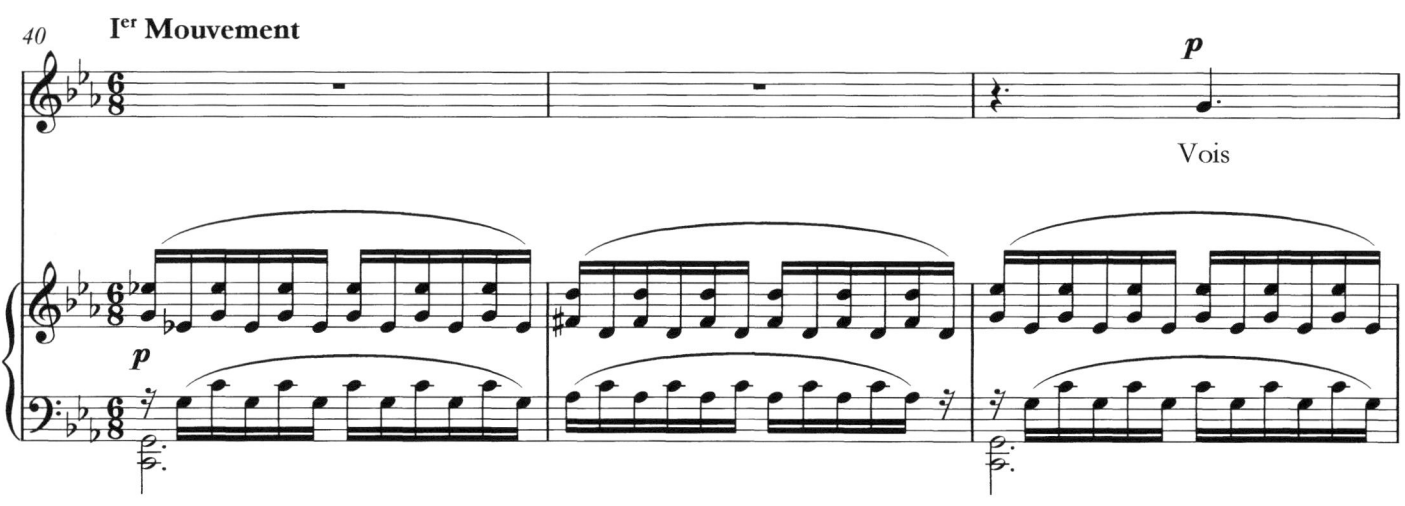

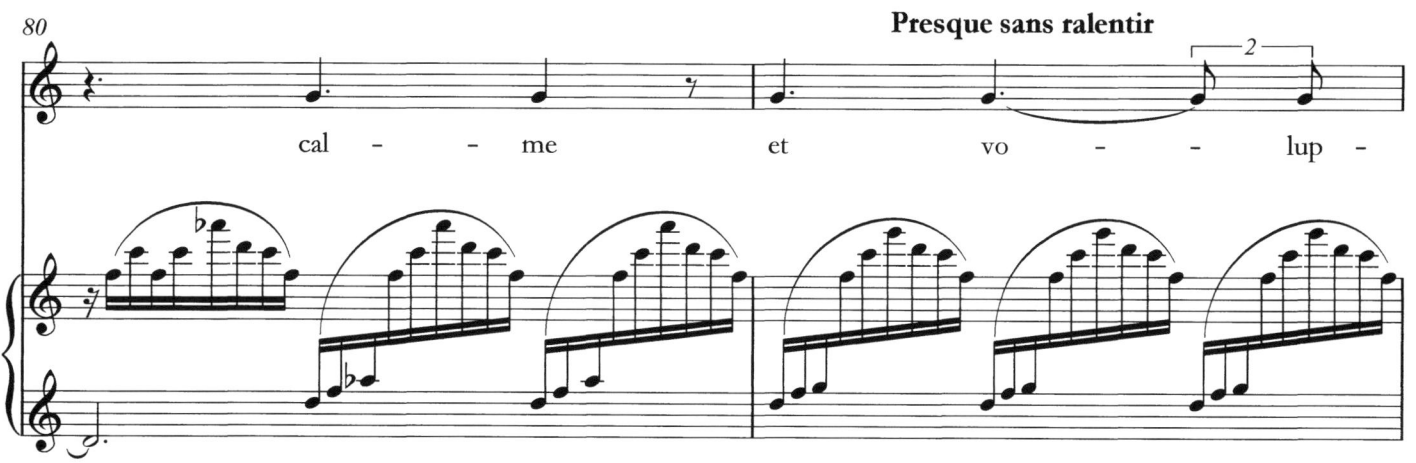

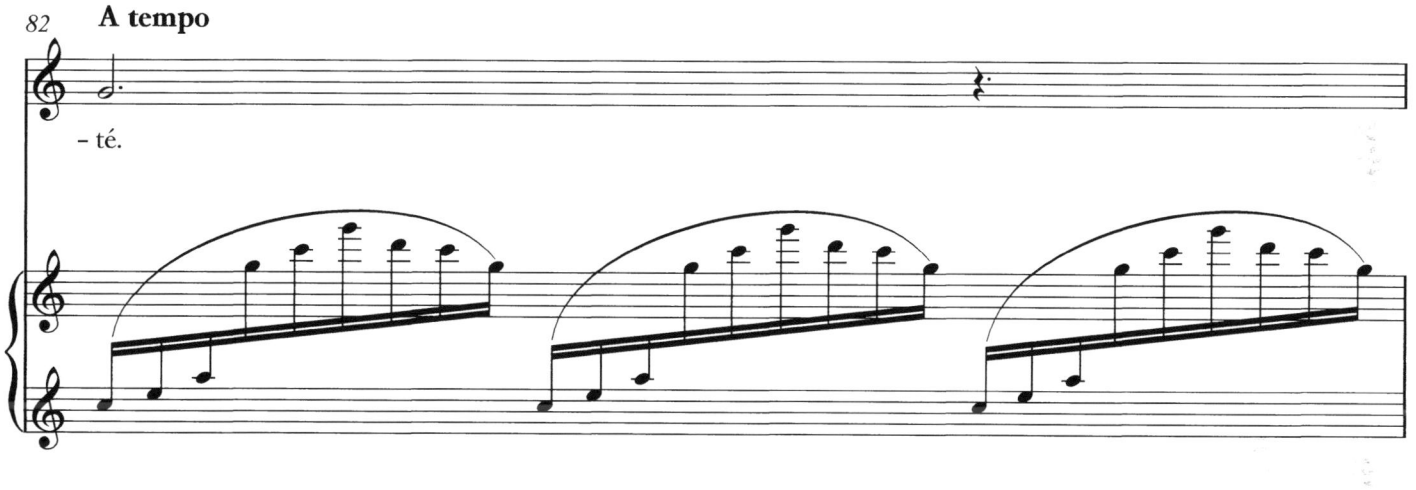

en diminuant (et en rallentissant toujours) jusqu'à la fin

à Monsieur Vincent d'Indy

8. La vague et la cloche
(Coppée)

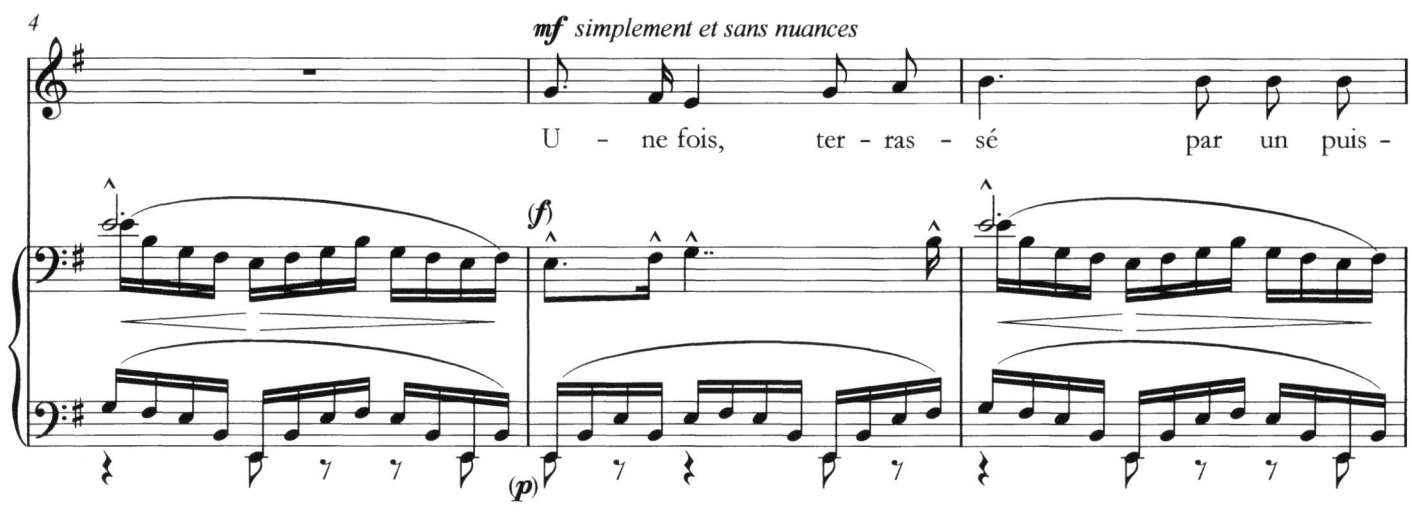

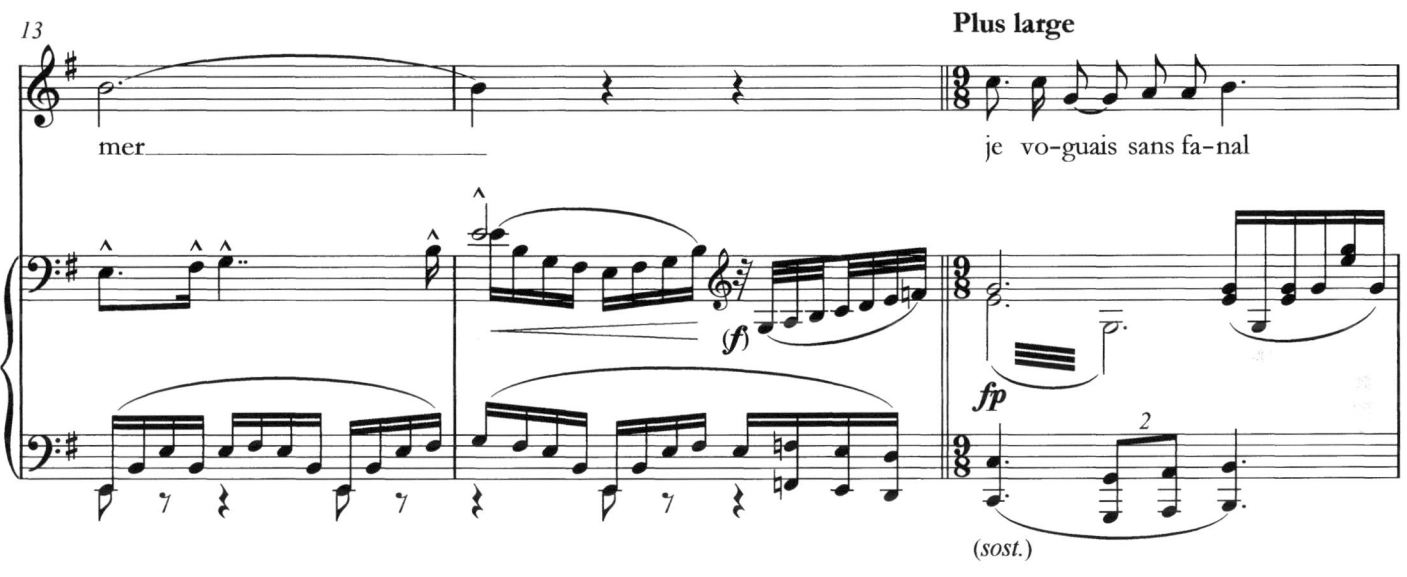
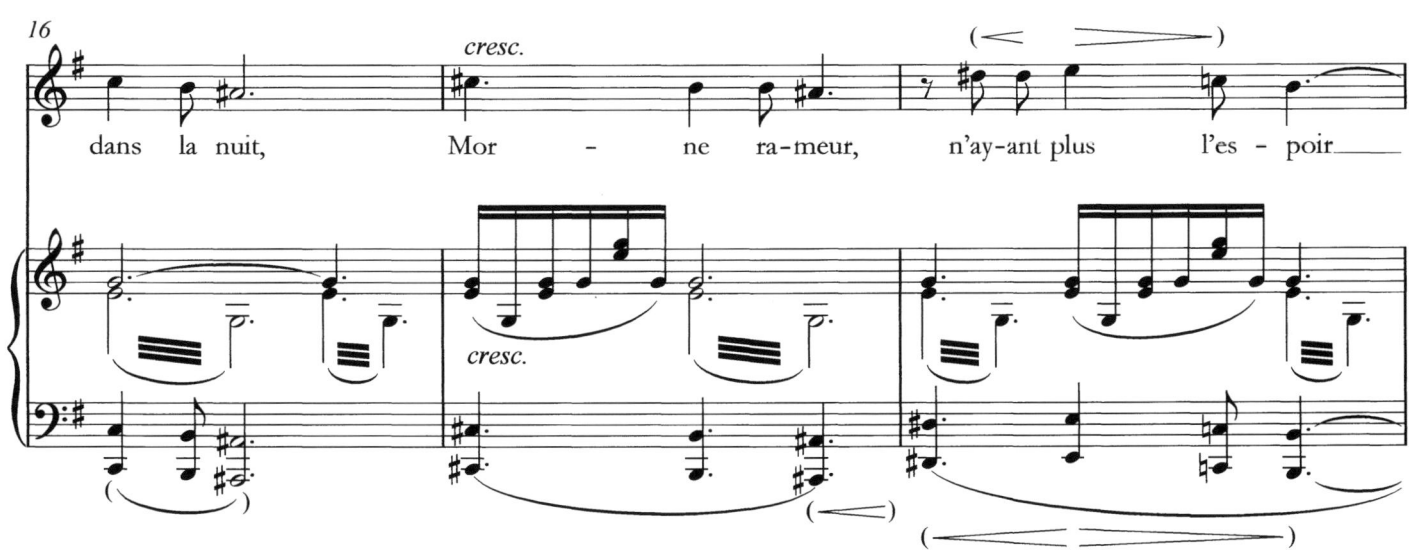

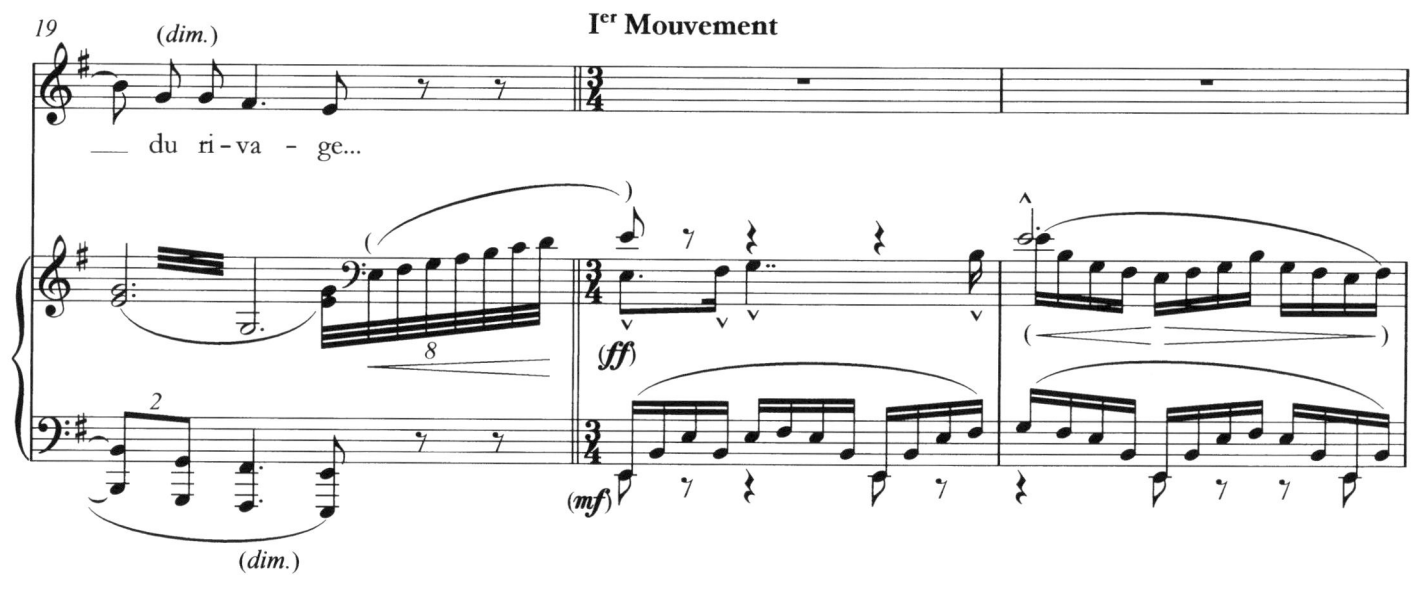
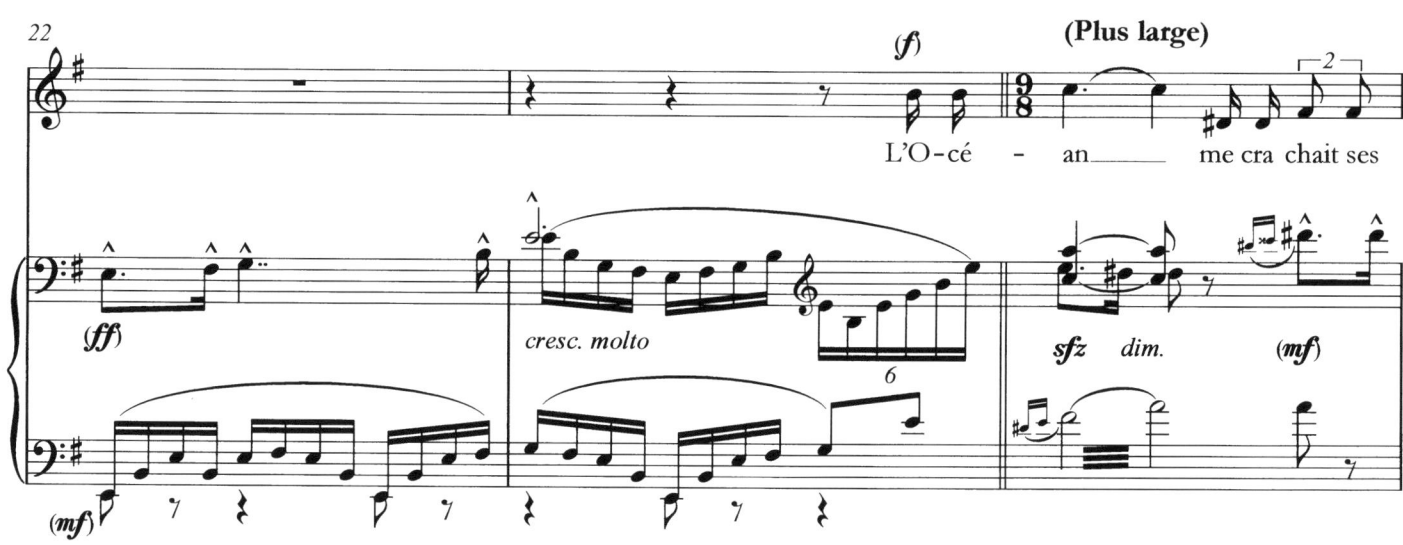

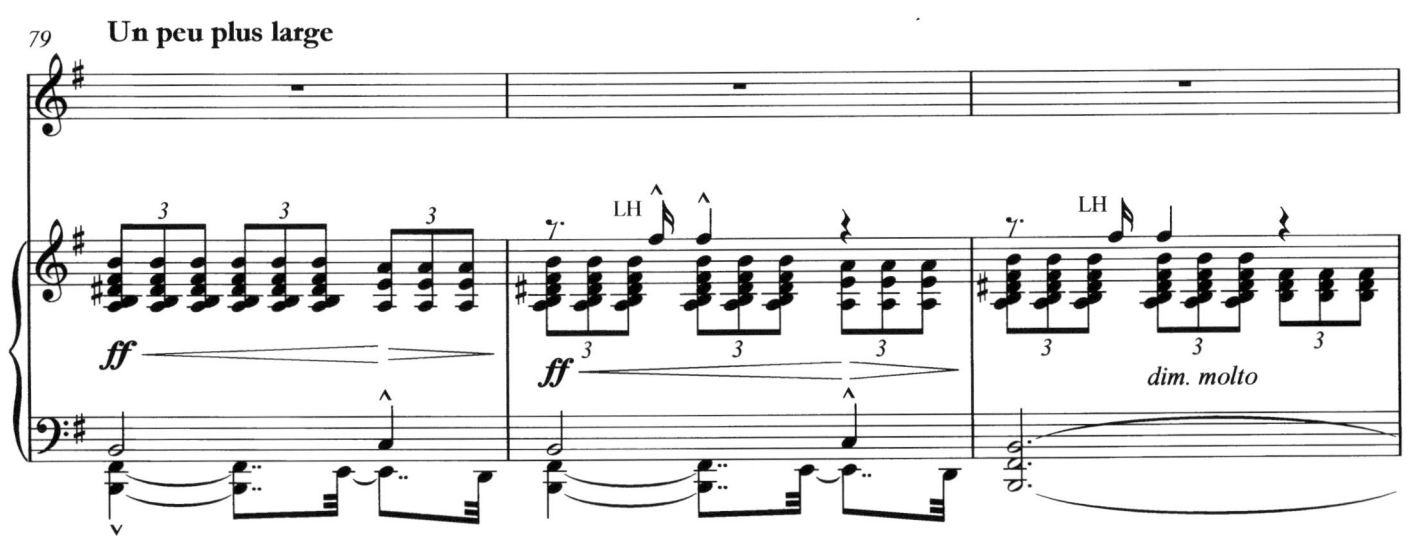

54

à la mémoire d'Henri Regnault
9. La fuite
(Gautier)

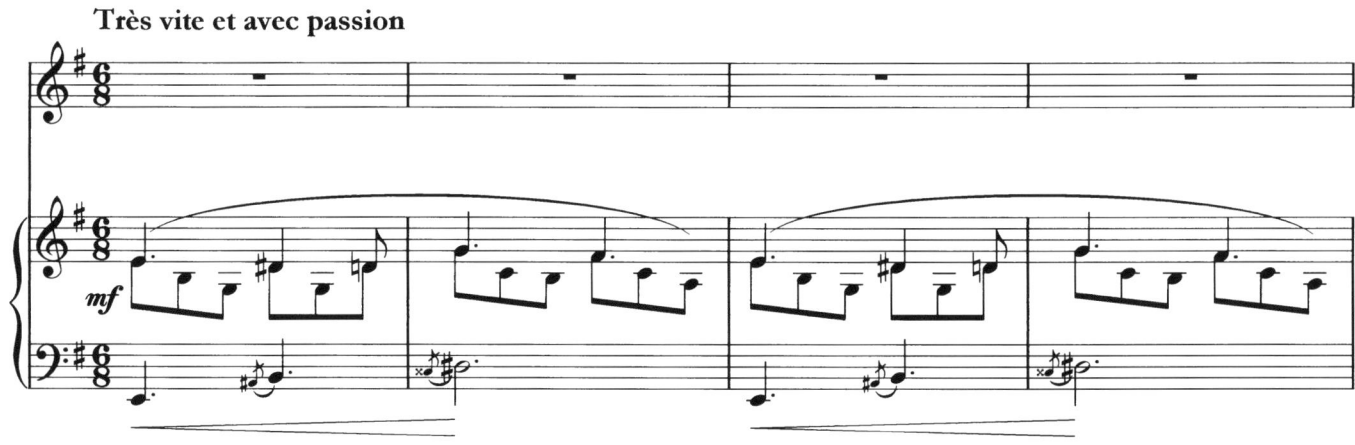

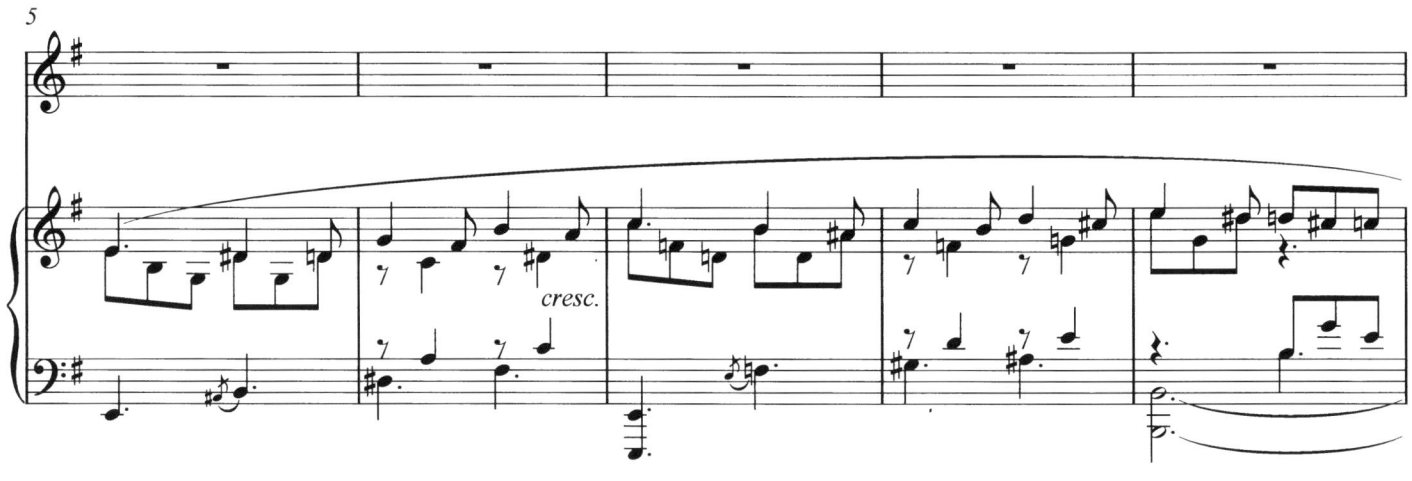

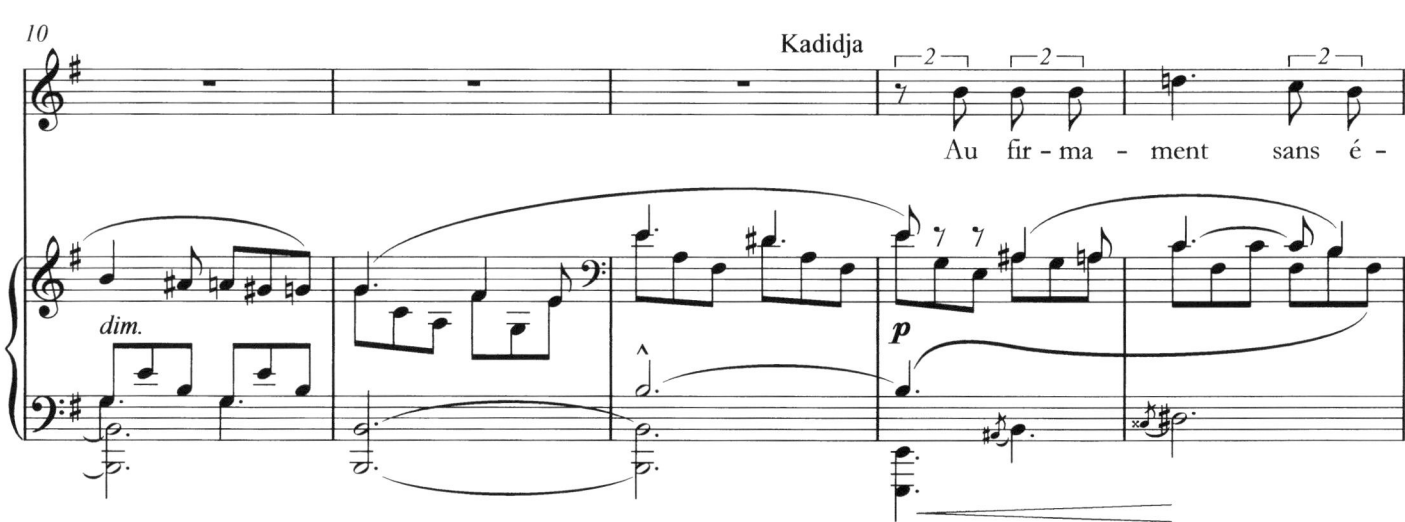

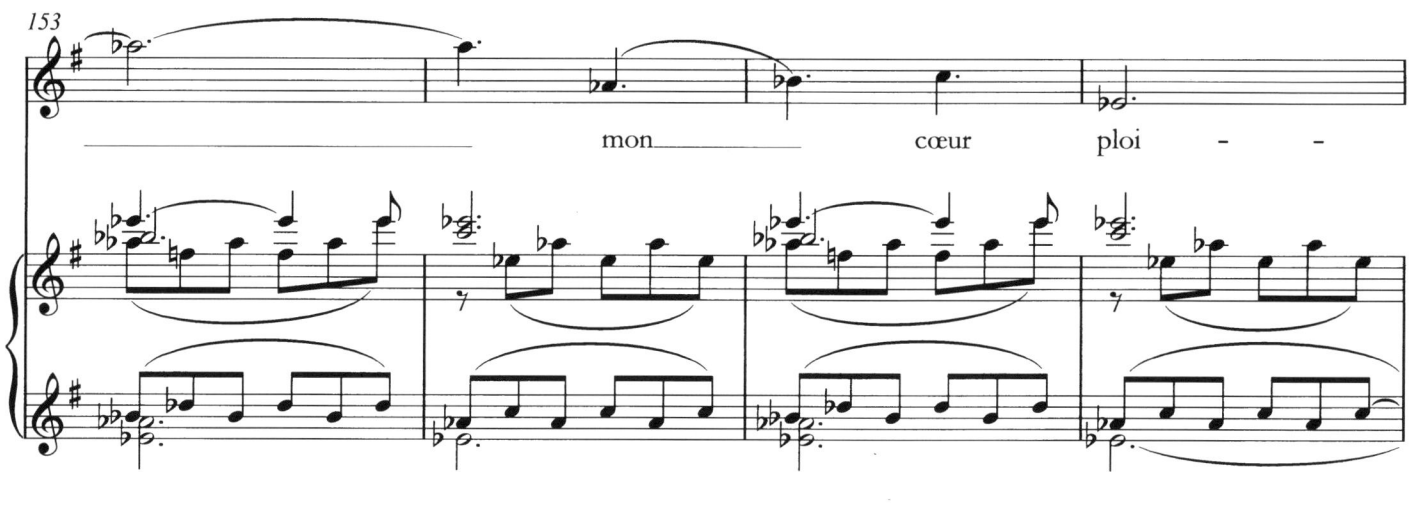

à la mémoire d'Henri de Lassus

10. Élégie

(Mme Henri Duparc, after Moore)

à Monsieur Henry Cochin
13. Sérénade florentine
(Lahor)

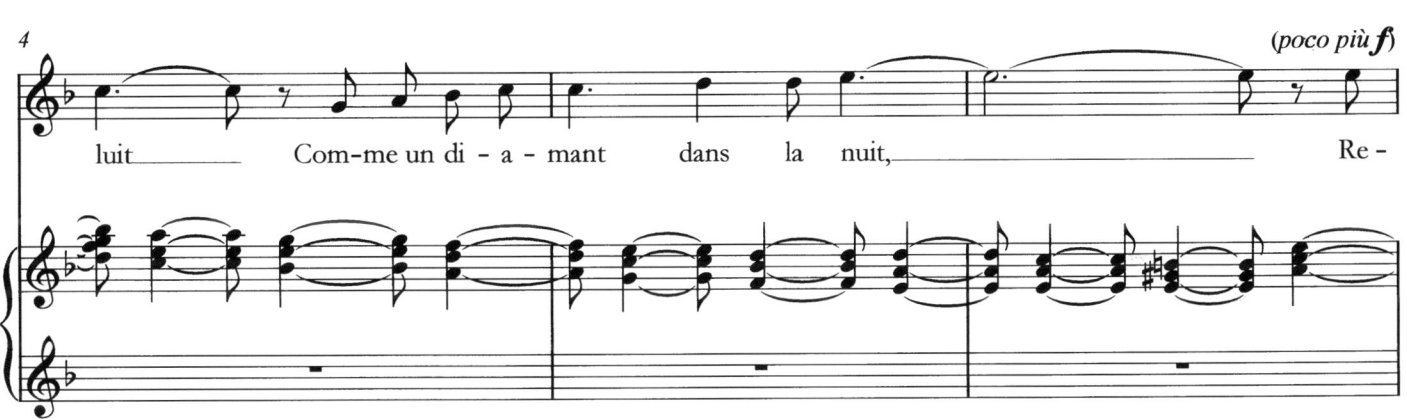

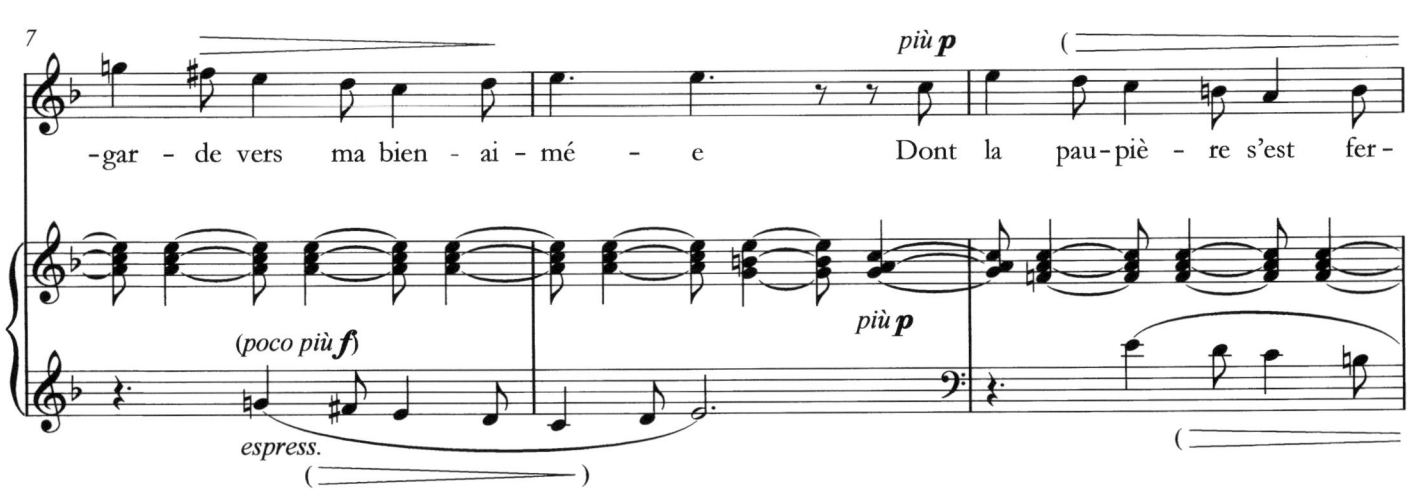

à Ernest Chausson

14. Phidylé

(Leconte de Lisle)

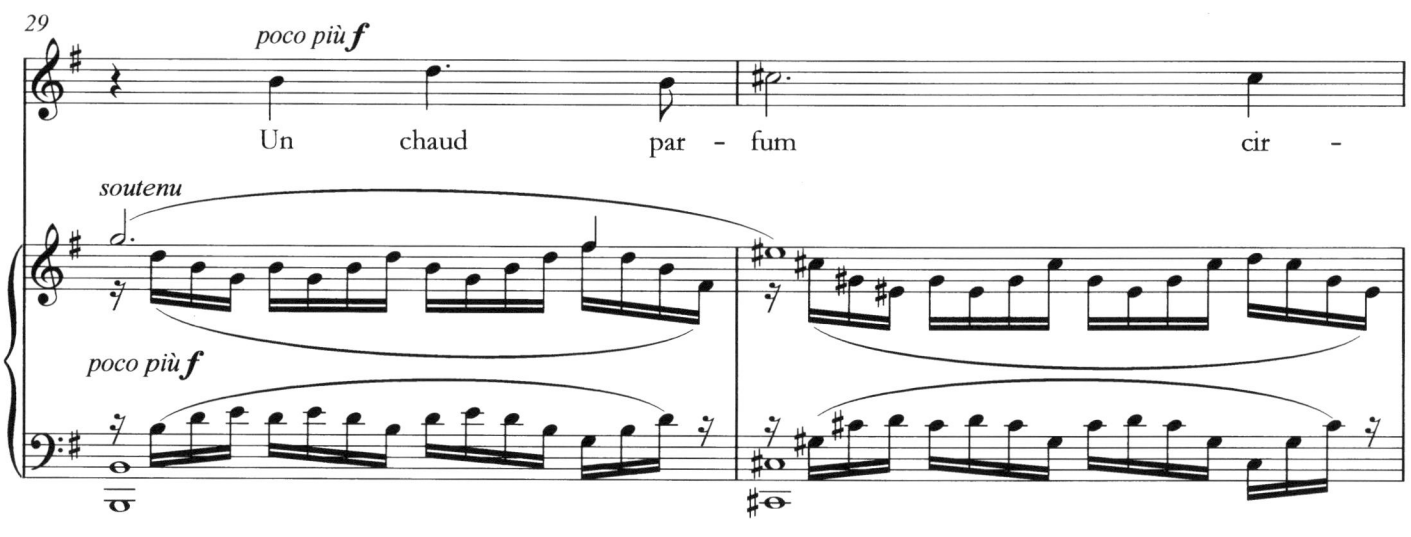

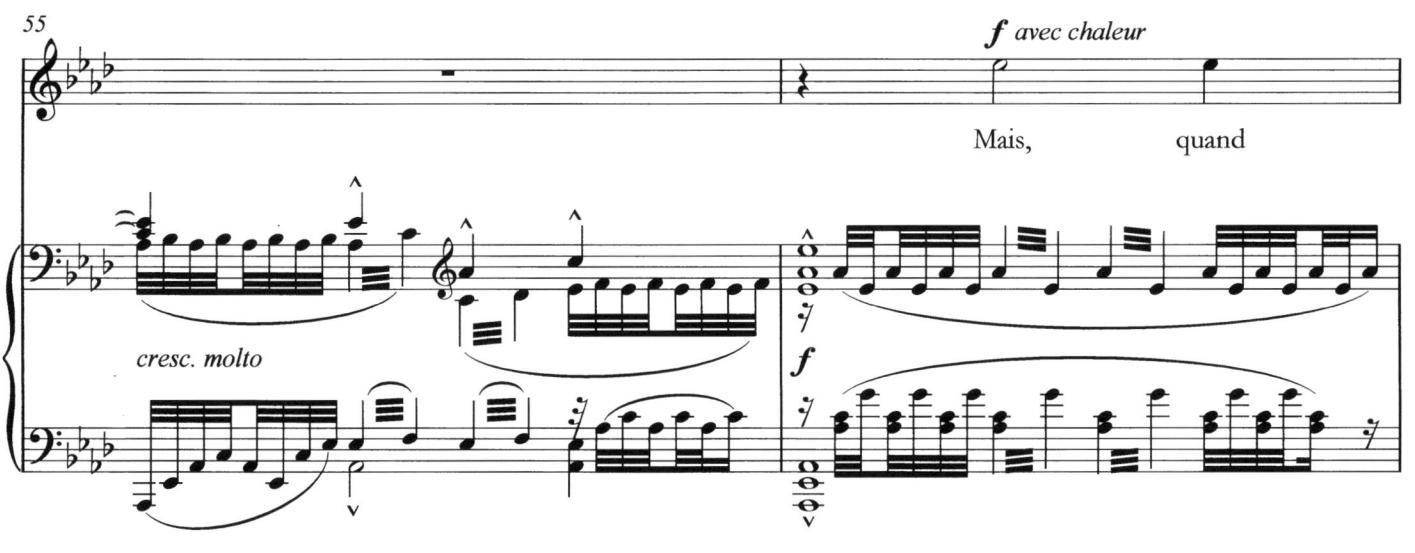

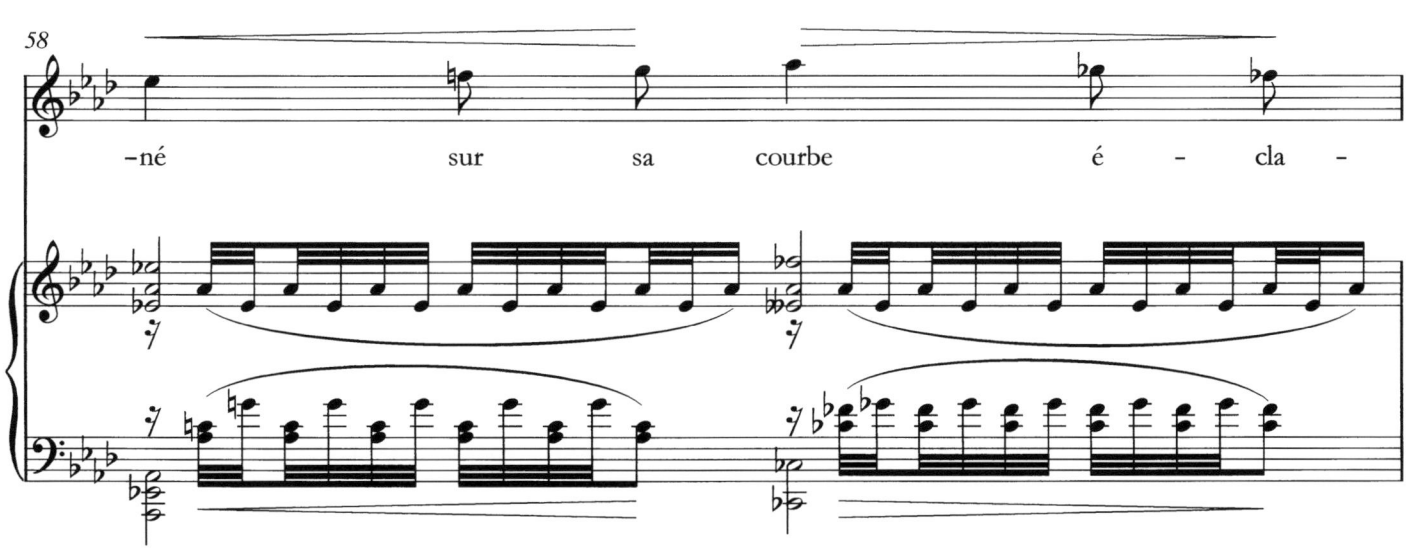

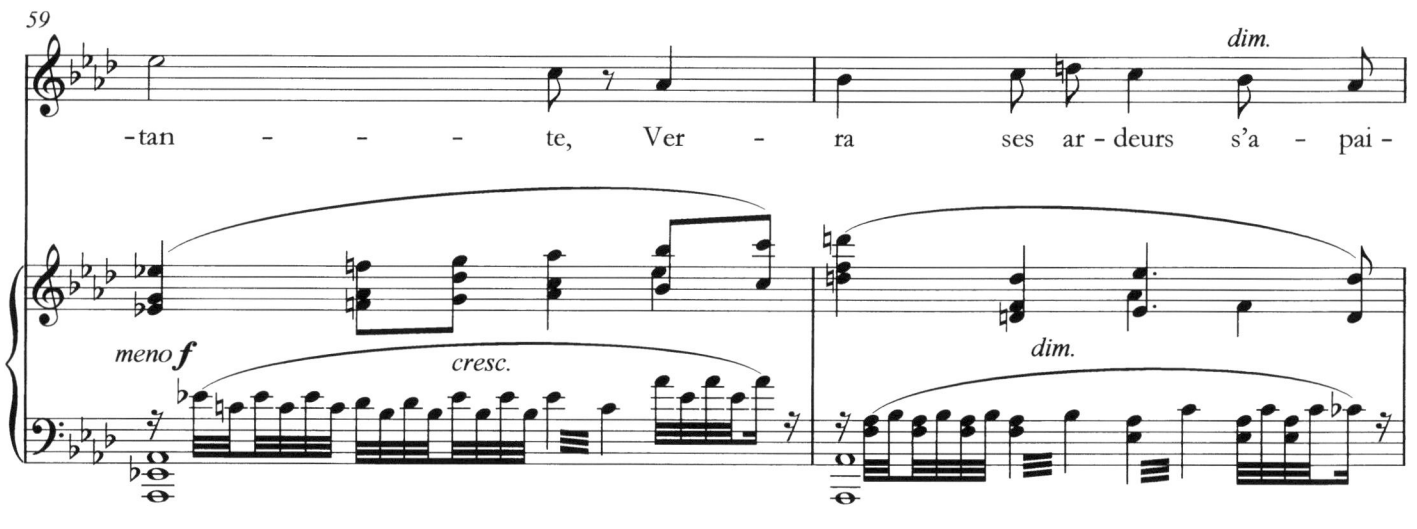

à Monsieur Gabriel Fauré

15. Lamento
(Gautier)

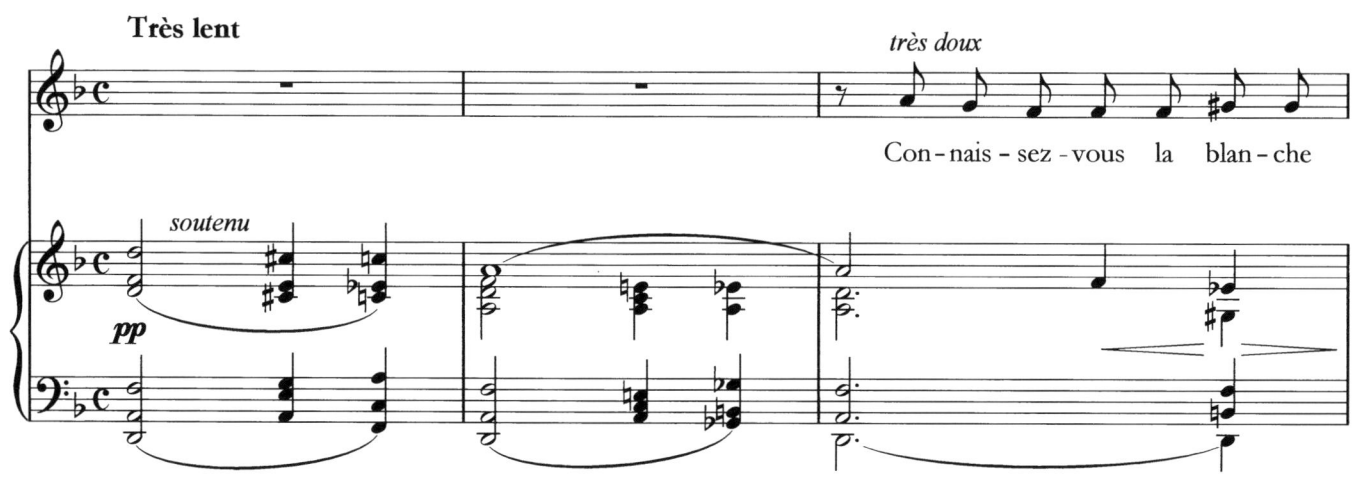

à Madame Henri de Lassus
(née Boissonnet)

16. Testament

(Silvestre)

Tou - te ma sè - ve s'est ta -

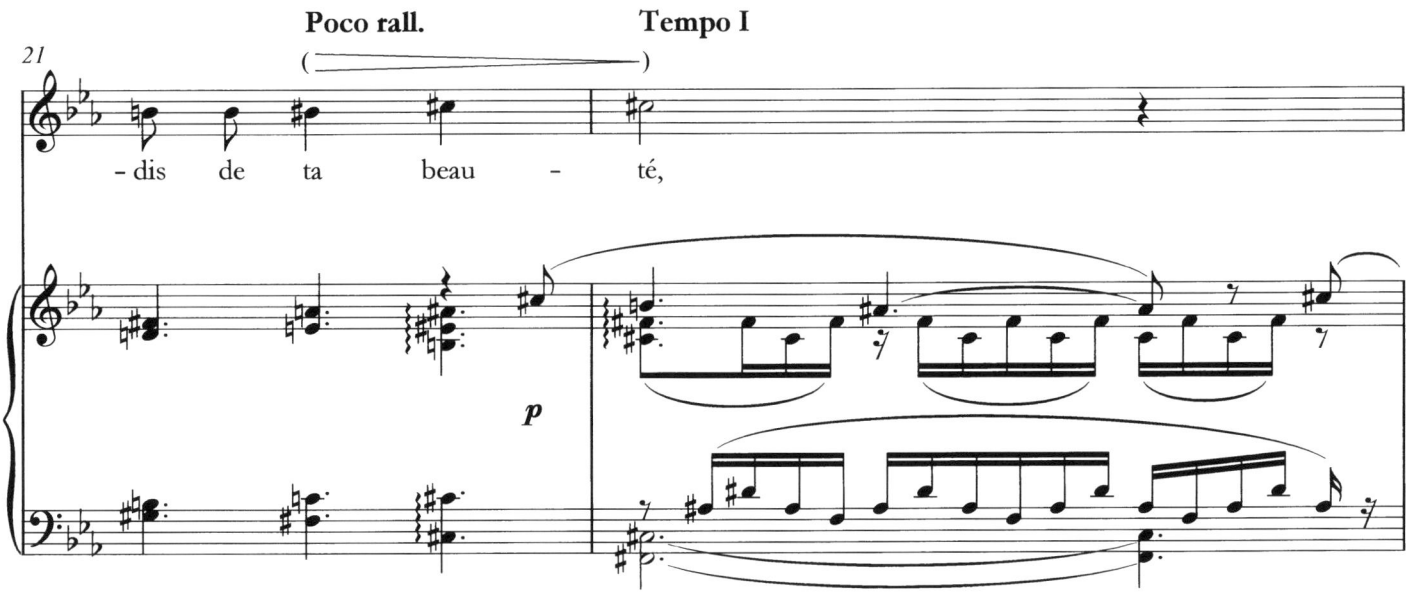

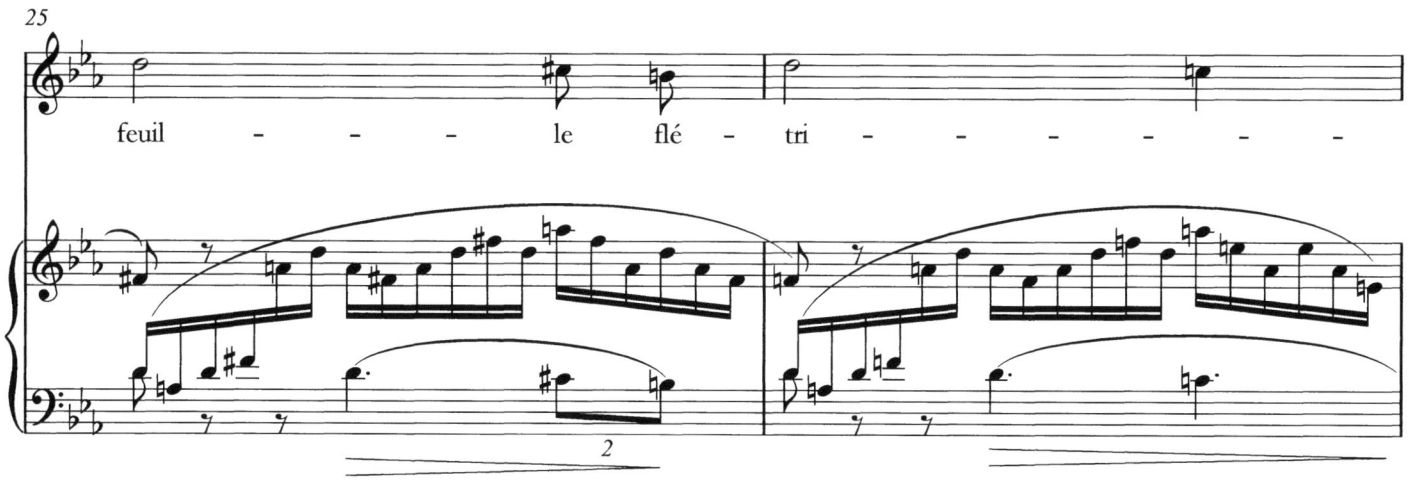

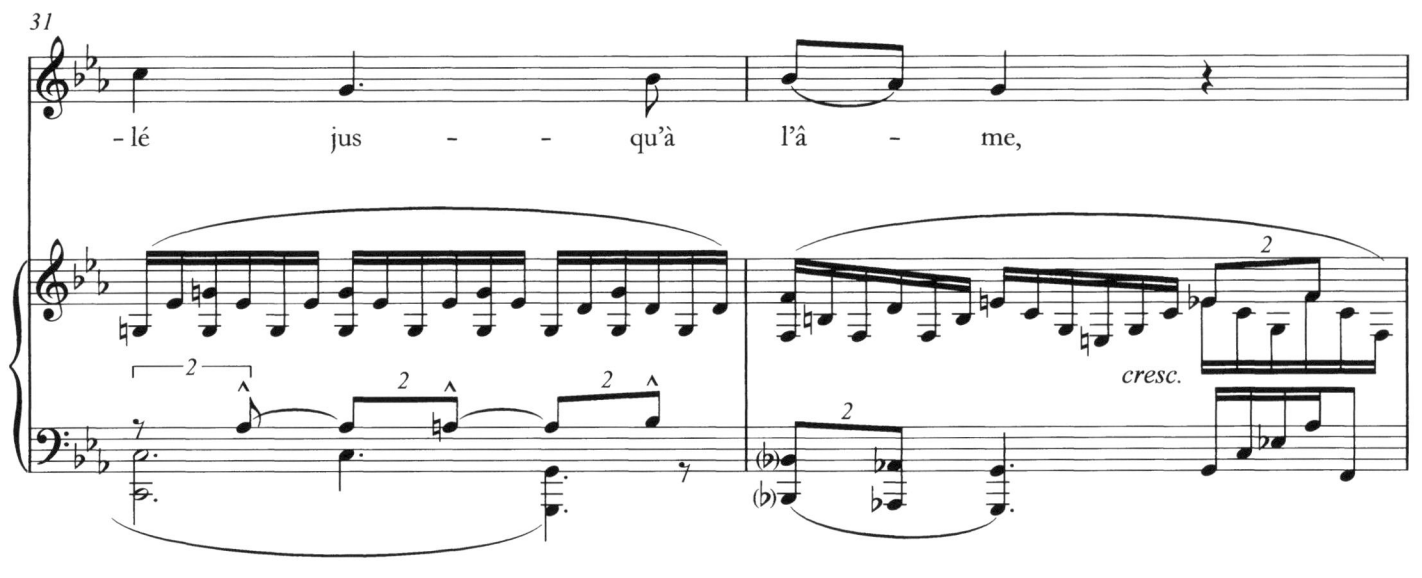
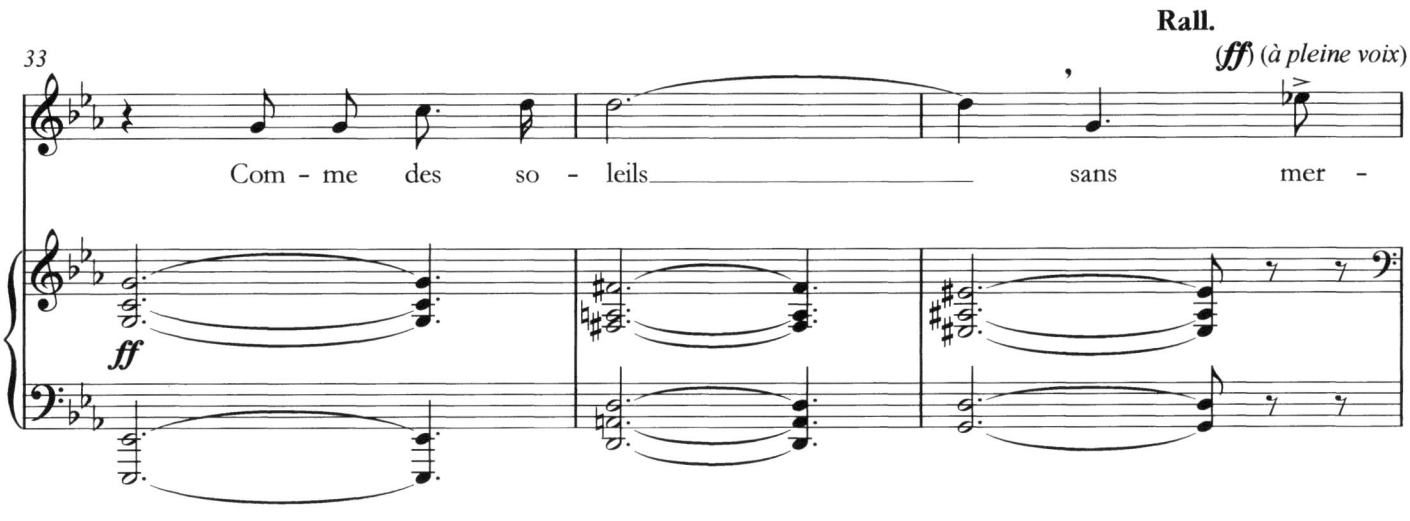

Mais a-

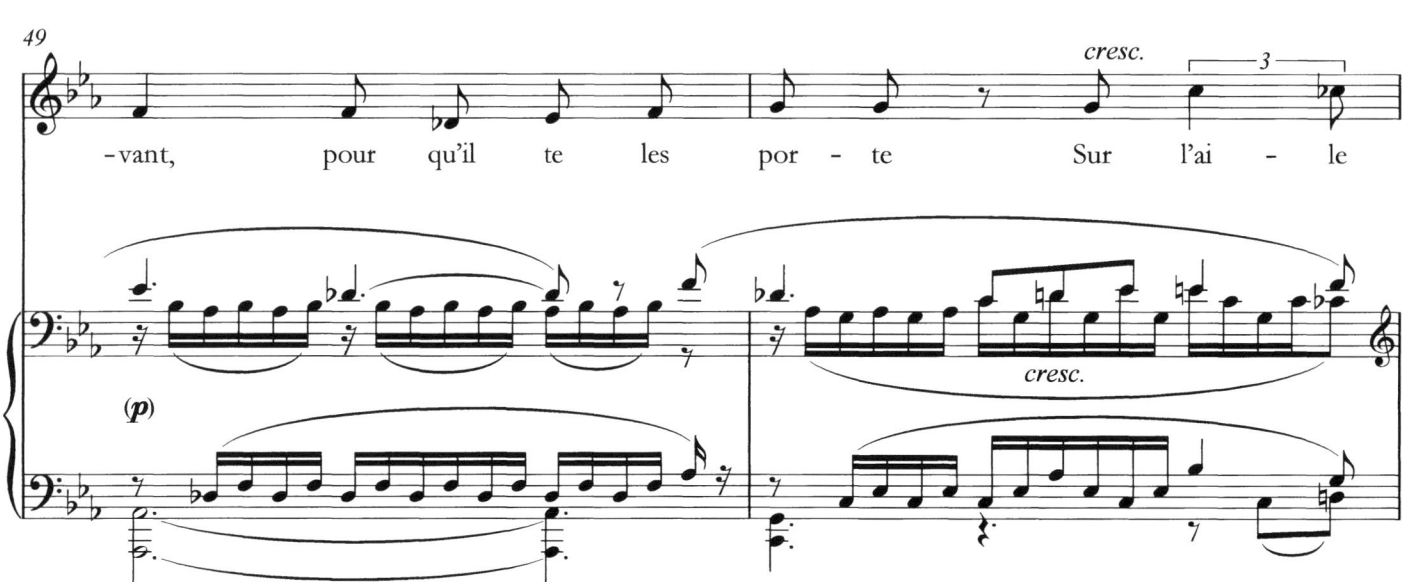

-vant, pour qu'il te les porte Sur l'ai - le

à Monsieur J. Guy Ropartz

17. La vie antérieure
(Baudelaire)

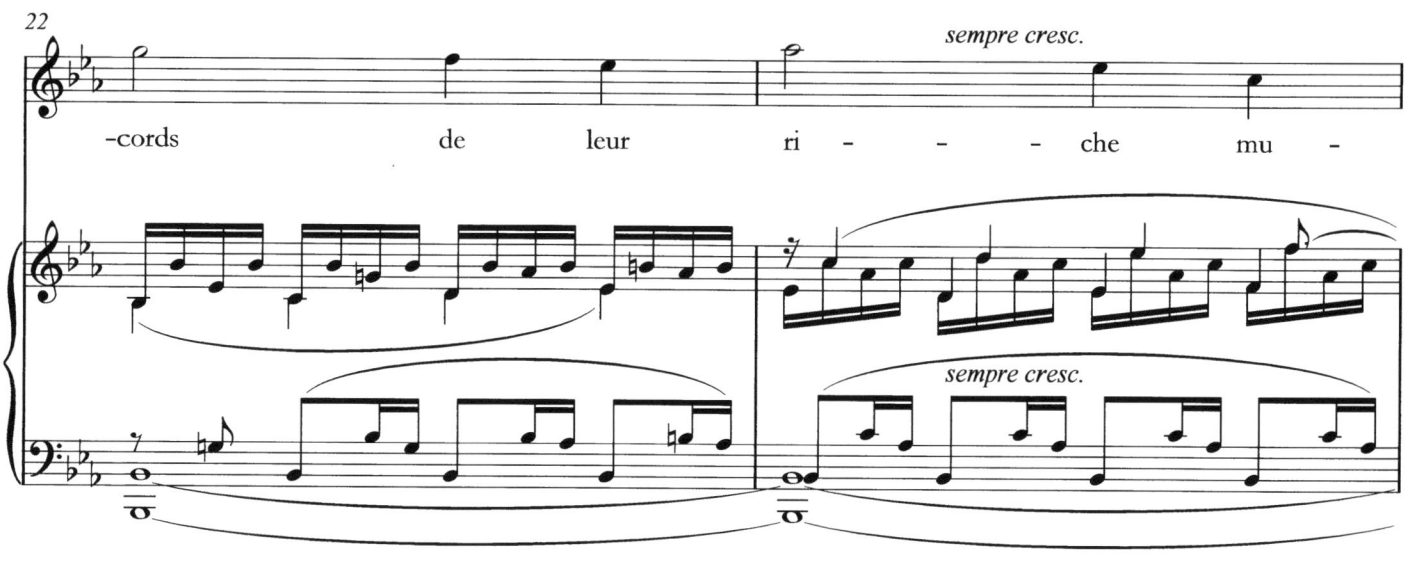

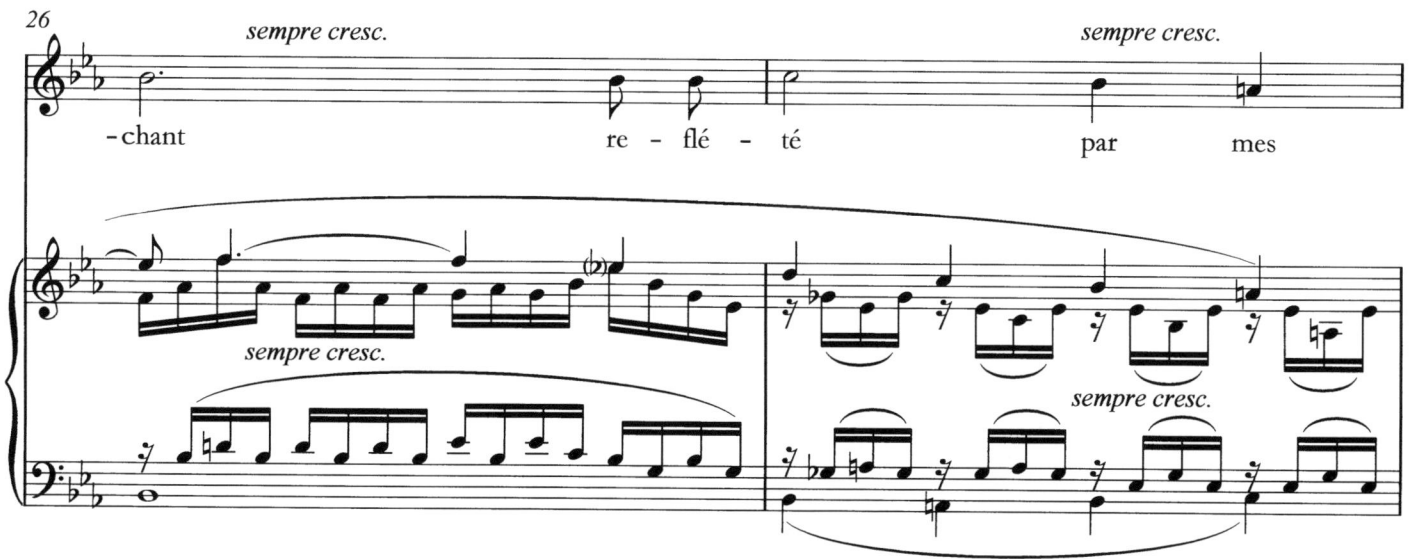

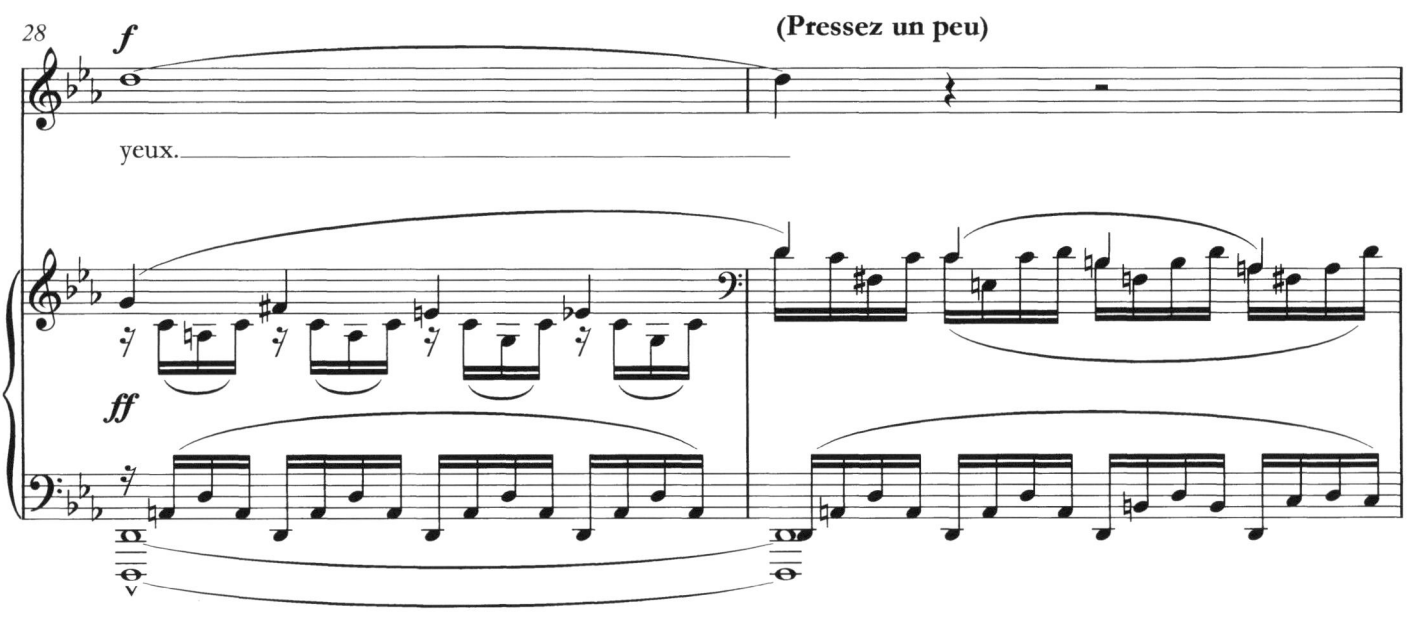

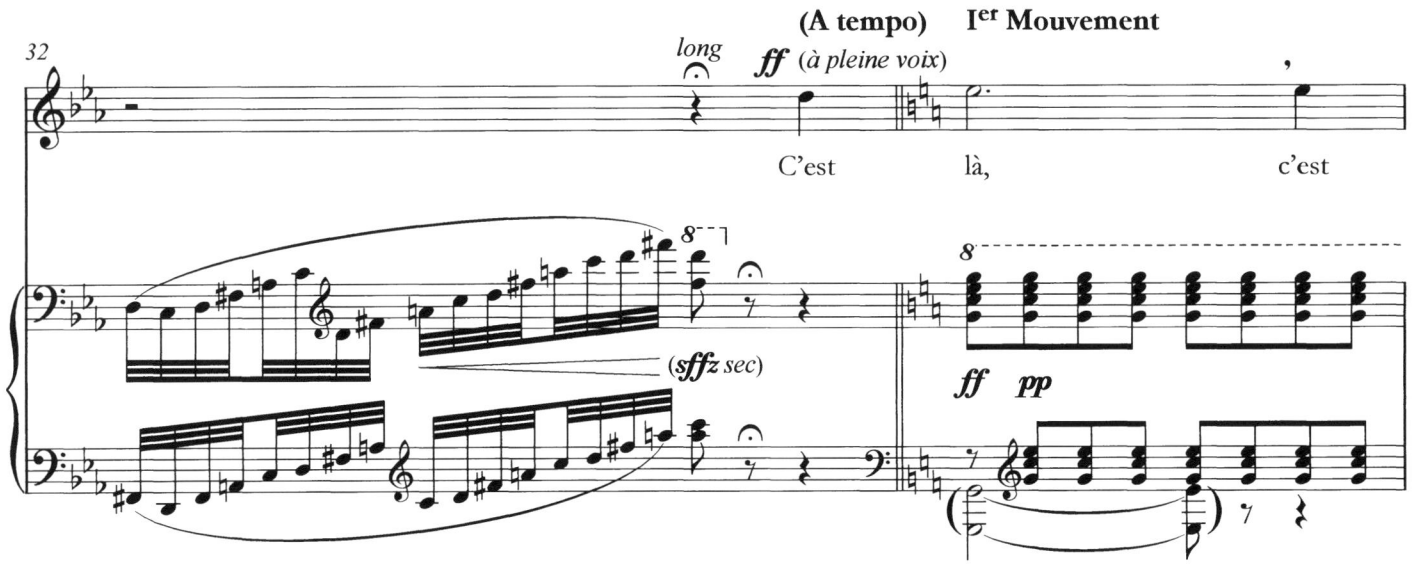

CRITICAL COMMENTARY

All the French texts and all the songs were first published in Paris.

The reference **E** is understood, where relevant, to comprise **E1**, **E2** etc. Similarly **E1**–**E3** will comprise **E1a**, **E1b**, **E2a**, **E2b**, and **E3a**, **E3b** respectively.

Abbreviations:
pf = piano   orch = orchestra
RH = right hand   LH = left hand
b(b)= bar(s)   p(p)= page(s)

The commentary uses the Helmholtz system of pitch nomenclature:

No. 1: *Chanson triste*

All editions dedicated *à Monsieur Léon Mac Swiney*
Poem by Jean Lahor (pseudonym of Dr Henri Cazalis, 1840–1909), from *Melancholia* (Lemerre, 1868), p49

Sources

A1 Autograph MS, 4pp, E♭ major, untitled, signed by composer, dated 18 août 69. bb1, 2, 11 and 12 are entirely lacking; vocal line is lacking in bb3, 4, 13 and 14. No indications of phrasing, articulation or pedalling, nor of dynamics except in b28 and b36, as noted below <d'Armagnac archives>

A2 Autograph MS, 4pp, E♭ major, signed at end by composer "H.D.", undated. bb1–4 and bb11–14 are entirely lacking; vocal line is lacking in bb5, 6, 15, 16. Indications of phrasing, articulation and dynamics, but not of pedalling. This MS was used for engraving of first edition (**E1**, see below) <d'Armagnac archives>

A3 Autograph MS, 5pp, E♭ major, unsigned, undated. This MS was used for engraving of second edition (**E2**, see below). The first page is reproduced in L. Rohozinski, ed., *Cinquante ans de musique française* (Paris, 1925), II, p20. Held in same folder is an autograph MS of first page of a transposition down to C major, conforming with version of **E2** for medium voice <Editions Salabert>

A4 Autograph MS of orchestral score, 12pp, E♭ major, unsigned, undated. This manuscript was used for engraving of edition (**E4**, see below) <Editions Salabert>

A5 Three autograph sketches for piano version of bb23 and 24, on last page of MS of *Soupir* (see below, **A1**)

E1a First edition, E♭ major, *5 Mélodies*, Op. 2 No. 4 (G. Flaxland, 1869; G.F. 1221 – later taken over by Durand, Schoenewerk et Cie)

E1b First edition, as above; this song with autograph envoi from the composer, dated 'janv. 1870' <BnF Cons. Rés. 2685>

E2a Second edition, as a separate item (E. Baudoux, 1901; E.B. et Cie 746)

E2b Transposition down to C major for medium voice (E.B. 747)

E3a Complete edition of *mélodies* (Rouart, Lerolle et Cie, 1911; A.R.5746.L & Cie)

E3b Transposition down to C major for medium voice (A.R.5747. L & Cie)

E4 Orchestral score by the composer (Rouart, Lerolle et Cie, 1912; R.L. & Cie 9818)

The first performance was given at the 77th concert of the Société Nationale on 2 March 1878 by Eugénie Vergin, the wife of the conductor Edouard Colonne. The first performance of the orchestral version was given at the Concert Lamoureux on 26 February 1911 by Hélène Demelliez, with Camille Chevillard conducting.

A4, **E4**: metronome mark, ♩=52
E1: *Andantino*
A1, **A2**: LH, dotted minim bass notes absent throughout

b1	**E1**: *p*. **A3**, **E2**, **E3**: *pp*
bb1, 2	**E1**: 𝄢. marked from beginning to end of each bar; no pedal marked in other sources
b2	**A3**: *très doux* omitted. **E1**: RH, semiquavers 5 and 17, *d′* instead of *e♭′*
bb3, 4	**E1**: beats 3 and 4, *decrescendo*; vocal line, phrasing marks between *e♭″* and *c″*, and *c″* and *b♭′* at beginning of b4. **A1**, **E1**: RH, internal resolutions (*f′*– *e♭′*, etc.) absent, and passim
b5	**A1**, **E1**: RH semiquaver 5, *e♭′* present
b6	**A3**: pf, beat 3, *poco cresc.* (not *poco rit.*)
b8	**E1**: vocal line, beats 1–3, *diminuendo*; beats 2–3 in **A2**. **E1**, **A2**: phrasing marks between *g″* and *e♭″*, and *e♭″* and *f′*
b9	**A2**, **E1**: vocal line, beat 2, *crescendo* to beat 3, *diminuendo* to beat 4
b10	**A1**, **A2**, **E1**, **E2**, **E3**: beat 4, semiquavers 3 and 6, *e♭′*, *e♭*; **E4**: *e♮′*, *e♮*
b12	**E1**: vocal line, beats 1 and 2, phrasing marks between *d″* and *g′*, *g′* (dotted crotchet) and *e♭″*; beat 3, *diminuendo* to end of bar; pf, beat 3, C minor
b13	**E1**: vocal line, beat 3, *p*, *diminuendo* to beat 4. **A4**, **E4**: beat 3, *poco rit.*
b14	**E1**: vocal line, beat 1, *p*, beat 2, *cresc*. **A4**, **E4**: beat 1, *pressez un peu*
b16	**E1**: vocal line, beat 1, *diminuendo* to beat 2; phrasing mark, beat 2 to beat 3. **A4**, **E4**: beat 1, *1° Tempo*
b17	**A1**, **A2**, **A4**, **E1**, **E4**: vocal line, beats 2–4, lower option only. **A3**, **E2**, **E3**: both options. **A2**: beat 2 to beat 3, *diminuendo*; **A2**, **E1**: vocal line, beat 2 to beat 3, phrasing mark
b18	**A2**, **E1**: *pp*
b20	**A2**, **E1**: vocal line, beat 1, phrasing mark from *f″* to *b♭′*; beat 3, phrasing mark to end of bar and *crescendo*
bb20–21	**A4**, **E4**: solo cello line, beginning on beat 3, inserts *e′* dotted crotchet before countermelody of **E2**, **E3**
b21	**A2**: vocal line, beats 3 and 4, *diminuendo*. **A2**, **E1**: phrasing mark, *a″* to *c♯″*
bb21–23	**A4**, **E4**: RH, long single phrase (b21, quaver 9 to b23, quaver 4) broken up into 4 shorter ones
bb21–24	**A1**: harmony and vocal line solidly in G♭ / D♭ major, but later version pencilled in by Duparc
b22	**A2**, **E1**: vocal line, beat 2, *crescendo* to beat 3, *diminuendo* to beat 4. **E1b**: RH, beat 1, quaver 3, *c♯″*; beat 3, quaver 3, *d♯″*

b23	**A2**, **E1**: vocal line, beat 2, first note, *crescendo* and phrasing mark up to $a\natural''$, then *diminuendo* and phrasing mark down to $c\sharp''$
bb23, 24	**A2**, **E1**: different harmonies. **A3**: different vocal line, but accompaniment of b24 essentially identical with printed text: both bars scored through in blue pencil. **A5**: these three sketches show that Duparc was always happy with vocal rhythm of these two bars as finally printed, but had trouble with melodic line and with harmonies
b24	**A2**, **E1**: RH, beat 2, first note a''; beats 3, 4, *dimin. molto*
b25	**A2**, **E1**: pf, beat 1, *dim.* absent; beat 3, ***pp***. **A2**, **A3**, **E1**: ***p***
bb25, 26	Repetition of the words 'une ballade' made by Duparc
b26	**A2**, **E1**: vocal line, beat 3, quaver 3, *crescendo*
bb26–27	**A2**, **E1**: vocal line, phrasing mark from last quaver of b26 to first note of b27
b27	**A2**, **E1**: beat 1, quaver 3, *poco rit.* absent; beat 2, phrasing mark from f' to bb' on beat 3. **E1**: vocal line, beat 2, *crescendo* up to beat 3, then *diminuendo* to beat 4
b28	**A1** and all subsequent sources: *très doux*. **A2**, **E1**: vocal line, beats 1 to 2, phrasing mark; no countermelody in RH. **A2**: vocal line, *diminuendo* through beats 1 and 2; **E1**: through beat 2. **E4**: countermelody, on solo cello and 1st horn, *expressif*; cello ***mf***, horn ***p***
b29	**A2**, **E1**: vocal line, beats 1 to 2, phrasing mark
b30	**A2**, **E1**: vocal line, beats 1 to 2, *diminuendo*; beat 2, note 1, g'; beat 4, $c\natural''$ over A♭ major arpeggio
b31	**A2**, **E1**: vocal line, beats 2 to 4, *diminuendo*; LH, beat 2, bottom F' absent
b32	**A2**: vocal line, last word, 'tristesses', copied in error from previous line. **A1** and all other sources: 'tendresses'. **A1**, **A2**, **E1**: RH, beats 2 to end of bar, all semiquavers single notes. **E4**: vocal line, crescendo extended to end of 'tendresses'
b33	**A2**, **E1**: vocal line, beats 1 to 2, *diminuendo*; pf, ***p***. **E4**: vocal line, beat 3, quaver rest followed by crotchet for 'je'; all other sources: dotted crotchet. Duparc wrote of this passage to Pierre de Bréville on 31 May 1923 that the piano version must 'se conformer exactement à la partition d'orchestre'. <BnF Lettres autographes Duparc (H.), 104>
bb34–36	**A1**, **A2**, **E1**: RH, chromatic countermelody absent
b37	**A1**, **A2**, **E1**: LH, bottom $E\flat'$ absent

No. 2: *Soupir*

Poem by René-François Sully-Prudhomme (1839–1907), known as Sully Prudhomme, from *Les solitudes* (Lemerre, 1869), p113

Sources

A1 Autograph MS, 3pp, D minor, signed by the composer 'H.D.' and dated at end 'Beaulieu, Oct. 69'. Dedication *à ma mère* has been crossed out in red pencil. It would seem that this MS was used for engraving of first edition, since it bears publisher's reference G.F. 1209. It is accompanied by cover of printed copy, on which there is a note by the critic M.-D. Calvocoressi: 'Manuscrit autographe de la première version (Octobre 1869) Ce manuscrit m'a été donné par l'auteur, le 4 mai 1902'. On verso of p3 are three sketches for bb23 and 24 of *Chanson triste* <BnF Cons. Ms. 12539>

A2 Autograph MS, 3pp, D minor, unsigned and undated. Dedication *à ma mère* has been restored. Dr van der Elst surmises that, after the death of Duparc's mother in 1895, the dedication of this melancholy song became relevant in a way that it had not been in her lifetime. This MS once belonged to the critic Charles Malherbe and was used for the 1901 edition, with the reference no. 750. <BnF Mus MS 1270>

E1 First edition, D minor, *5 Mélodies* Op.2 No. 1 (G. Flaxland, 1869; G.F. 1209 – later taken over by Durand, Schoenewerk et Cie)

E2a Second edition, as a separate item (E. Baudoux, 1901; E.B. et Cie 750)

E2b Transposition down into B minor for medium voice (E.B. et Cie 751)

E3a *Mélodies, nouvelle édition complète* (Rouart, Lerolle et Cie, 1911; A.R.5750.L & Cie)

E3b Transposition down into B minor for medium voice (A.R.5751.L & Cie)

The first performance was given at the 8th concert of the Société Nationale on 9 March 1872 by Catherine Miquel-Chaudesaignes or E. Bertrand

	A2, **E2**, **E3**: dedicated *à ma mère*
	A1: *Andante*. **E1**: *Quasi andante*. **A2**, **E2**, **E3**: *Lent*
	A2, **E2**, **E3**: *Lié et soutenu*
b1	**A1**, **E1**: tenor g' held for minim, resolving on to quaver f', in tenths with top part; quavers 5, 6, no tie on alto a'
bb1, 2	**A1**: quaver 3 to quaver 5, *diminuendo*
bb1, 2, 3	**A1**: accents on quaver 2 in tenor part, and in b3 in top part
bb4, 7	**A1**, **E1**: tenor g' as in b1
bb4, 8	**A1**, **E1**: no tie on alto a', as in b1
b9	**A1**, **E1**: vocal line, beat 1, quaver plus quaver rest; beat 2 to quaver 6, *crescendo* and *diminuendo*; RH, beat 3, d'', e'' absent. **A1**, **E1**: RH, beat 3, accents on alto bb', g'
bb10, 11	**A1**, **E1**: vocal line, *crescendo* from b10, beat 2 to beat 6, then *diminuendo* to b11, quaver 3; breath marks absent
b11	**A1**, **E1**: vocal line, beat 2, quaver plus quaver rest; accpt., top part, $e\sharp''$ absent, plain A7 chord; *poco rall.* absent
bb12, 13, 14	**A1**, **E1**: LH, quaver 6, tenor part, d' instead of $c\sharp'$
bb14, 15	**A1**, **E1**: LH, bass, two dotted minim D's
bb16–21	**A1**, **E1**: pf figuration largely different
b16	**A1**, **E1**: B♭ major harmony
bb16–18	**A1**, **E1**: LH, bass, three dotted minim F's
b18	**A1**: vocal line, *crescendo* marked earlier, on beat 1
b19	**A1**, **E1**: vocal line, beat 1, ***f***; beat 2 to quaver 6, *diminuendo*; LH, lower octave notes absent
b21	**A1**, **E1**: beat 3, *diminuendo*; RH, top part, $g\natural'$
b22	**A1**, **E1**: ***pp***
bb22–26	**A1**, **E1**: RH 8ve up
b24	**A1**, **E1**: vocal line, ***mf***; pf, *più **f*** absent
bb27–37	**A1**, **E1**: this passage, originally of 9 bars, entirely rewritten and extended in **A2**, **E2**, **E3**
b38	**A1**: vocal line and pf, *très doux*
b39	All sources: vocal line, beat 1, dotted minim, in error for minim. Corrected editorially
b43	**A1**, **E1**: vocal line, beat 1, quaver plus quaver rest; breath mark absent; beat 3, accents on quavers. **A1**: *crescendo* and *diminuendo* through bar; beat 2, *ritard.*

b44	**A1**, **E1**: vocal line, beat 1, accent on dotted crotchet
bb44–45	**E1**: vocal line, b44, quaver 4 to b45, beat 2, *crescendo* and *diminuendo*
b45	**A1**, **E1**: vocal line, beat 2, semiquaver plus semiquaver rest; beat 3, *rit.* and *crescendo*. **A1**: quaver 6, *diminuendo*
b46	**A1**, **E1**: LH, quaver 6, *eb'*
b48	**A1**, **E1**: LH, *D* added to printed chord (and chord spread); vocal line, 'Toujours!' on crotchet and minim *a*'s; voice and pf, ***ppp***. Repetition of the word 'Toujours' comes from the composer
b49	**A1**, **E1**: this bar absent

No. 3: *Romance de Mignon*

Poem by Victor Wilder, based on the first two verses of Goethe's ballad *Kennst du das Land*

Sources

A Autograph MS, 4pp, E major, entitled *Mignon. mélodie Pour voix de Soprano*, signed by composer, with autograph dedication: *Hommage reconnaissant à Madame Mac Swiney, (en souvenir de l'excellente soirée que j'ai passée chez elle le jeudi 15 avril.69)*. From collection of Charles Panzera <BnF Mus MS 20771>

E First edition, E major, *5 Mélodies*, Op. 2 No. 3 (G. Flaxland, 1869; G.F. 1194 - later taken over by Durand, Schoenewerk et Cie)

The date of a first performance during the life of Duparc is unknown.

A is only partially supplied with dynamic and articulation markings. Otherwise, the following are points of interest:

A: *Lento, con tenerezza*. **E**: *Quasi lento*
E: dedication, *à mon ami Arthur Coquard*

b13, 15, 21, 23, 59, 61, 67, 69	pf and voice, *cresc.* and *dim.* hairpins not aligned, this follows Duparc's notational preference
b26	**A**, **E**: vocal line and RH, quaver 6, ♮ missing from *d'''* and *d'*. Supplied editorially
b47	**A**: second verse identified as *2e Couplet*
b66	**A**: vocal line, dotted minim. **E**: augmentation dot omitted
b72	**A**: vocal line and RH, quaver 6, ♮ missing from *d'''* and *d'*. **E**: missing from *d'*. Supplied editorially
b98	**A**: RH, quaver 6, bottom note *d♯*. **E**: *f♯*. Present edition prints *d♯* as providing a smoother link to *c♯* in b99. But either reading possible

No. 4: *Sérénade*

Poem by Gabriel Marc, from *Soleils d'octobre* (Lemerre, 1869), p47

Sources

A Autograph MS, 3pp, G major, signed by composer 'H.D.', dated 'août 69' <d'Armagnac archives>. It was not possible to consult this MS. Remarks below are based on notes taken by Nancy van der Elst during her study of this source

M MS, 3pp, G major, non-autograph, undated <d'Armagnac archives>

E First edition, G major, *5 Mélodies*, Op. 2 No. 2 (G. Flaxland, 1869; G.F. 1211 – later taken over by Durand, Schoenewerk et Cie). Dedicated *A mon ami Noël Guéneau de Mussy*

The date of a first performance is unknown
Changes between **A** and **E** are mostly in adjusting weight of accompanying chords. Other changes include:

bb9–11	**A**: pf, dominant-tonic alternations. **E** introduces characteristic falling scale in the bass
b10	**A**: vocal line, quaver 3, *d♯'*. **E**: *c♮"*
b16	**A**: LH, quaver 4, *b*, supporting B7 chord. **E**: *G♯*. Duparc has replaced the poet's 'point' by 'pas'
b28	**A**: pf, semiquavers 2 and 8, *d* and *c* (in octaves with voice). **E**: *f* twice; vocal line, quaver 2, augmentation dot present in **A**, omitted in error in **E**
b40	**M** is identical with **E**, except for missing ♮ to pf *f'*
b41	Quaver 6, ♭ to *b'''* absent from all sources. Added editorially
b43	The pianist pauses on quaver three and holds while the singer reaches the last syllable of 'pleurer'; the pianist then moves on to quaver four while the singer pauses on that last syllable

No. 5: *Le galop*

Poem by René-François Sully-Prudhomme, known as Sully Prudhomme, from *Stances et Poèmes* (A. Fauré, 1869), p65

Sources

A Autograph manuscript, 6pp, G minor, signed and dated at end 'nov. 1869'. Headed *Le Galop Mélodie pour Voix de Basse*. This MS was used for engraving of first edition. On verso of p6, sketch for unidentified song. From collection of Claire Croiza <BnF Mus MS 19911>

E First edition, G minor, *5 Mélodies*, Op.2 No.5 (G. Flaxland, 1869; G.F. 1210 – later taken over by Durand, Schoenewerk et Cie).

Dedicated *à mon frère Arthur Duparc*

Readings from **A** are given in ( ) - see Preface

Durand et Cie published a second edition in 1948, 15 years after the composer's death, with the vocal line transposed into the treble clef, but otherwise unchanged except for the introduction of four misprints. This transposition has been followed in the high voice edition

The first performance was given at the 118th concert of the Société Nationale on 11 March 1882 by Numa Auguez

b25	**A**, **E**: RH, quaver 1, ♭ missing before *e"*; supplied editorially
bb30–32	**A**: b30, beat 3 to b32, beat 3, *dimin.*
b43	**A**: *energico* marking absent
bb44–47	**A**: all dynamic markings absent
b49	**A**, **E**: LH, ♯ wrongly applied to *B*; reapplied editorially to *d♯*
b50	**A**: marked *bien rhythmé* (sic); vocal line, beat 3, *ab* accented
b51	**A**: vocal line, beat 3, *ab* accented
b70	**A**: vocal line, beat 4, wrongly written as *a*; **E**: corrected to *g♯*
b76	**A**, **E**: RH, beat 4, ♭ missing before *e'*; supplied editorially
b83	**A**: vocal line, beats 3, 4, *crescendo*
b87	**A**: vocal line, *crescendo* through whole bar
b93	**A**, **E**: RH, upper note, *f♭'''*; corrected editorially to *f♮"*
b97	LH phrasing added editorially
b98	**A**, **E**: LH, beat 4, ♯ missing before *f*; supplied editorially
b99	**A**, **E**: RH, beat 2, ♮ missing before *e'*; supplied editorially

No. 6: *Au pays où se fait la guerre*

Poem by Théophile Gautier (1811–1872) entitled *Romance*, from *La Comédie de la Mort* (Dessessart, 1838), p221

Sources

A1 Autograph MS, 3pp, F minor, headed *Absence. Mél pour mezzo-Soprano*, signed at end, undated, with autograph pencil corrections <BnF Cons.MS. 9853>

A2 Autograph MS, 5pp, F minor, signed next to title, *Au pays où se fait la guerre*, and at end, undated. Initial dedication *à mademoiselle Eugénie Vergin* crossed out and replaced by *à Madame Colonne* (her married name) <BnFMus MS 1268>

A3 Autograph MS of orchestral score, 19pp, F minor, headed *Au pays où se fait la guerre*, signed, undated. This MS was used for engraving of printed orchestral score (**E4**, see below) <Editions Salabert>

E1 First edition (early version), F minor, headed *Au pays où se fait la guerre*, as supplement to *Journal de musique*, ed. Armand Gouzien, I, No 51, 19 May 1877

E2 Second edition (Rouart, Lerolle et Cie, 1910; R.L. & Cie 9735)

E3 Final version, in *Mélodies, nouvelle édition complète* (Rouart, Lerolle et Cie, 1911; R.L. & Cie 9735)

E4 Orchestral score by the composer (Rouart, Lerolle et Cie, n.d. [1913]; R.L. 9924 & Cie)

Although **E2** and **E3** have the same plate number, Duparc did make some small changes in the later edition, as noted below.

The first performance was given at the 8th concert of the Société Nationale on 9 March 1872 by Madame E. Bertrand, under the title *Romance*. The first performance of the orchestral version was given at the 55th concert of the Société Nationale on 1 April 1876 by Eugénie Vergin, with Edouard Colonne conducting, under the title *Absence*.

Duparc made important comments about the structure of the song in a letter of January 1911 to Mme Troyon in Montrémy: 'Vous avez bien tort de vous inquiéter du caractère dramatique de la mélodie *Au pays où se fait la guerre* et qui, dites-vous, convient moins à votre nature – vous n'y cherchez que trop un caractère dramatique – ce que je veux, et surtout, [est] un sentiment de rêverie désolée qui ne devient dramatique qu'à la fin à partir de ces mots : "quelqu'un monte à grands pas la rampe". Jusque là, ce n'est que triste, mais sans impatience, une tristesse résignée. Vous dites très bien le morceau : accentuez le contraste entre les deux premières strophes et la troisième et ce sera parfait.' ('You are wrong to be worried about the dramatic character of the song *Au pays où se fait la guerre*, which, you say, does not really suit your personality – you are looking too hard for a dramatic character in the song – what I want, above all, is a feeling of desolate reflection which does not become dramatic until the end, from the words: "quelqu'un monte à grands pas la rampe". Up until that point it is merely sad, but without impatience – the sadness of resignation. Your declamation of the song is excellent: accentuate the contrast between the first two verses and the last and it will be perfect.') I am grateful to Nancy van der Elst for providing a transcript of this letter.

All editions: curiously, these still carry dedication *à Mademoiselle Eugénie Vergin*

A1:	*Andante* absent
A1, **A2**, **E1**:	no metronome mark
bb7, 8	**A1**, **A2**, **E1**: LH, merely repeated c' minims
bb12–15	**A1**, **A2**, **E1**, **E2**: vocal line, higher option absent
b13	**A1**, **A2**, **E1**: vocal line, beats 3 and 4; appoggiaturas c', eb', quavers db', c'. **E2**: appoggiaturas db', eb', quavers db', c'. **A3**, **E3**, **E4**: appoggiaturas omitted, quavers eb', db'. **A1**: quaver 3, *rall.* **A2**: *poco riten.*
b14	**A1**, **A2**, **E1**: ⌢ over minim. **A1**: beat 2, *A tempo*
bb14, 15	**A3**, **E2**, **E3**, **E4**: these 2 bars expand single bar of earlier sources, which may explain absence of a ⌢
b15	**A1**, **A2**, **E1**: vocal line enters on beat 2, necessitating repetition of 'Il semble'
bb21, 22	**A1**, **A2**, **E1**: pf, various different versions of contrapuntal movement over dominant pedal
bb32, 36	**A1**, **A2**, **E1**: LH, octave c / C, no tenor db'/ab dyad
bb41–43	**A2**: RH, variant countermelody
b45	**A3**, **E4**: vocal line, beat 2, c'' only. All other sources, c' with optional c''. See b91
bb46, 47	**A1**, **A2**, **E1**: vocal line, compressed version of bb12–15; pedal F continued from b45
b47	**A3**, **E4**: pf, ⌢ over quaver on beat 2, followed by ⌢ over quaver rest
b53	**A3**, **E4**: metronome mark, ♩=84
bb57–69	These bars underwent extensive revision through various stages. 'Cooing of doves' in pf, bb59–60, does not appear until **E2**
b65	**A3**, **E4**: vocal line, dotted crotchet and quaver; breath mark after dotted crotchet
b74	**A1**, **E1**: *poco cresc.*
b77	**A1**, **E1**: *très doux*
b78	**A1**, **E1**: *pp*
b81	**A1**, **A2**, **E1**: vocal line, quaver 1, c''
b85	**E1**, **E2**: vocal line, beat 1, db' quaver tied back to minim in b84; RH, db' crotchet similarly. **A1**: c'' quaver in vocal line against db' crotchet in LH
bb85, 86	**A1**: vocal line enters on beat 2, necessitating repetition of 'Et moi'
b86	**A1**: beat 2, *rall.*
b87	**A1**: beat 1, *più lento.* **E1**: *poco più lento*
b89	**A2**: vocal line, quaver 4, *crescendo* to crotchet in b90; *diminuendo* to quaver 3
b90	**A1**: beat 2, *poco rall.* **E1**: *rall.*
b91	**A3**, **E4**: vocal line, beat 2, crotchet c''. See b45
b92	**A1**, **A2**: vocal line, ornamented as in b13, except that **E2** now follows earlier versions
bb92, 93	**A1**, **A2**, **E1**: LH, pedal F continued from b91. **E2**: LH line eb', db', c' absent
b93	RH, beat 2, pianists with small hands may prefer to take bb' quaver with LH
bb94–107	**A1**, **A2**, **E1**: first 4 bars of song repeated at this point. 14 bars of 'Plus vite' section originally only 9, with shorter (F minor) lead-in and lead-out. No 5-note 'agitation' motif
bb108–122	**A1**, **A2**, **E1**: basic shape of final version plainly discernible, with many differences of detail and timing
b115	**A1**, **A2**, **A3**, **E4**: *volez*. **E1**, **E2**, **E3**: *voilés*; *volez* unclearly written in **A1**
b122	**A1**, **E1**: vocal line, beat 2, *avec élan*
bb123, 124	**E1**: vocal line, *portez la voix* (from ab'' to ab')
b124	**E1**: vocal line, beat 2, *crescendo*
b125	**E1**: vocal line, *dim.*

b126	**A1**, **E1**:	vocal line and LH, quaver 1, *c″*. **E1**: vocal line, quaver 4, *f*
b129	**A2**, **E1**:	RH, *bb′* ties between quavers 2 and 3, not quavers 1 and 2. Given prevalence of pedal, probably not significant except insofar as weight of quaver 3 is reduced
bb130, 131		
	A1, **A2**:	vocal line enters on beat 2, necessitating repetition of 'Et moi'
bb135, 136		
	A1: *rall.* **A2**, **E1**: *rall. e dim. molto*	
b136	**A1**:	vocal line, beat 2, quaver *c′*. **A2**, **E1**: crotchet *c′*
b137	**A1**, **E1**: *très lent.* **A1**, **A2**, **E1**: vocal line, *vibrato*. **A3**, **E4**: *rall. molto*	
bb137, 138		
	A1, **A2**, **E1**:	vocal line, crotchet *c′*, appoggiaturas *c′*, *eb′* to quaver *db′*, minim *c′*
b138	**A3**, **E4**:	pf, ⌢ over quaver on beat 2, followed by ⌢ over quaver rest
b139	**E1**: *pp*	
bb139, 140		
	E1: 𝄢. through b139, released at start of b140; similarly in bb141, 142	
bb140, 142		
	A3, **E4**:	beat 2, *crescendo* and *diminuendo* on chord in strings, not in woodwind
b141	**E4**: *pp*	
bb141–142		
	A1:	final appearance of motto at original pitch. **A2**, **E1**: as in bb139, 140
b142	**E2**, **E3**: *rall.* **A3**, **E4**: *rall.* absent	

No. 7: *L'invitation au voyage*

Poem by Charles Baudelaire (1821–1867), from *Les fleurs du mal* (Michel Lévy, 1868), p166

Sources

A1 Autograph MS, 8pp, B♭ minor, signed by composer, undated <Editions Salabert>

A2 Autograph MS, 5pp, B♭ minor, unsigned, undated <d'Armagnac archives>

A3 Autograph MS, 7pp, B♭ minor, with autograph dedication at end: *A Mademoiselle Croiza, souvenir de son amicable visite à Tarbes le 15 octobre 1914. H. Duparc* <BnF Mus MS 19912>

A4 Autograph MS of orchestral version, 20pp, C minor, unsigned, undated. This MS served for engraving of edition (**E3**, see below) <Editions Salabert>

E1a First edition, C minor (E. Baudoux, 1894, reprinted 1902; E.B. et Cie 60)

E1b Transposition down to A minor for medium voice (E.B. et Cie 738)

E2a *Mélodies, nouvelle édition complete*, C minor (Rouart, Lerolle et Cie, 1911; A.R. 5060. L. & Cie)

E2b Transposition down to A minor for medium voice (A.R. 5738. L. & Cie)

E3 Orchestral score, C minor (Rouart, Lerolle et Cie, n.d.; E.B. & Cie 343). There is also an orchestral version for medium voice, in A minor

The first performance was given at the 8th concert of the Société Nationale on 9 March 1872 by Catherine Miquel-Chaudesaigues. The first performance of the orchestral version was given at the 262nd concert of the Société Nationale on 18 May 1897; the singer was Maurice Bagès, the conductor probably Vincent d'Indy.

For information about choice of keys, see Preface p. v

E1, **E2**, **E3**:	dedication, *à Madame Henri Duparc*	
A4, **E3**:	metronome mark, ♩.=58	
bb2, 4, 6	**A4**, **E3**: pf, beat 2, *diminuendo*	
bb7, 8	**A1**, **A3**: vocal line, b7, quaver 3 to end of b8, *crescendo*	
b8	**A2**, **A4**, **E3**: *crescendo* through whole bar	
b14	**A1**, **A4**, **E3**: vocal line, beat 1, dotted crotchet; **A4**, **E3**: followed by breath mark. **A3**: vocal line, beat 2, crotchet *ab′*, quaver *g′*; this seems much weaker than the 1911 text, and is not printed here	
b20	**A1**: vocal line, beat 2, *p*	
b22	**A1**: vocal line, *crescendo* continued up to beat 1	
b23	**A4**, **E3**: vocal line, breath mark at end of beat 1; *dim.* omitted, and in orchestra	
b25	**A1**: *très articulé, avec une tendresse câline et un peu ironique* (clearly articulated, with a coaxing and slightly ironic tenderness). **A2**: *très articulé*	
bb26, 27	**A3**: vocal line, *diminuendo* extends to end of b27; **E2**, only to quaver 4. **A4**, **E3**: no *diminuendo*	
b27	**A3**: vocal line, quaver 3, *très articulé*	
b30	**A4**, **E3**: orchestra, *ppp*	
bb30, 31	**A4**, **E3**: vocal line, *portez la voix*	
b32	**A1**, **A4**, **E3**: after *Un peu plus vite, mais très peu*. **A4**, **E3**: ♩.=72	
b39	**A1**: pf, 'long' over and under ⌢ marks. **A4**, **E3**: pf, crotchet undotted, followed by quaver rest with second ⌢ mark	
bb40, 41	**A1**: *p* absent; *un peu moins doux que la première strophe*	
b45	**A3**: vocal line, quaver 6, *f′*	
b46	**A3**: vocal line, beat 1, crotchet, presumably with dot omitted in error, *crescendo* to beat 2. **A4**, **E3**: dotted crotchet, no *crescendo*	
b47	**A1**, **A3**, **A4**, **E3**: vocal line, *crescendo* through bar	
b48	**A4**, **E3**: *diminuendo* through bar	
b49	**A1**: *crescendo* through bar	
b50	**A1**: *avec plus de chaleur, mais sans presser*; LH, *en dehors* instead of *expressif*	
b53	**A4**, **E3**: *cresc.* (*molto* omitted)	
b55	**A4**, **E3**: *poco a poco dim.*	
b58	**A4**, **E3**: ♩.=76. Pianists may like to note orchestral dynamics: strings *p*; celesta (or typophone) *ff*; harp *f*	
b60	**A1**: vocal line, beat 1, dotted minim followed by breath mark	
b65	**A2**: beat 2, *dim.*	
b66	**A1**: vocal line, *crescendo* through bar. **A4**, **E3**: no dynamic markings from *più p* to end of song	
b67	**A1**: vocal line, *diminuendo*; hairpin in bb66 & 67 carries instruction *marquez bien la nuance*	
bb67–69	**A2**: b67, quaver 9 to b69, quaver 7, *cresc. poco a poco*	
b68	**A3**: vocal line, *crescendo* through bar	
b69	**A2**: vocal line, quaver 7, *più f*	
b71	**A4**, **E3**: pf, beat 3, *poco a poco dim.* brought back from b72	
b75	**A1**, **A2**, **A3**: LH, beat 2, *très en dehors*. **A3**: *cantabile* omitted	
b79	**A1**, **A3**: LH, *cantabile* absent. **A3**: *en dehors*; *ff* omitted. **A1**, **A2**: *très en dehors*	
b83	**A3**: beat 2, *En diminuant et en rallentissant toujours jusqu'à la fin*	
b87	**A3**: *rall.* (*molto*)	

No. 8: *La vague et la cloche*

Poem by François Coppée (1842–1908), from *Le reliquaire*, 1864–1866 (Lemerre, 1870), p29

Sources

A1 Autograph MS of original orchestral score, 23pp, E minor, *mélodie pour voix de basse et orchestre*, vocal line in bass clef, signed near title and at end, dedication: *à Monsieur Vincent d'Indy*, undated <BnF Mus MS 1271>

A2 Autograph MS of Duparc's piano reduction, 9pp, E minor, vocal line in treble clef, unsigned, undated. This MS was used for engraving of **E2** (see below) <BnF Mus MS 1272>

E1 First edition, E minor, vocal line in bass clef (E. Baudoux, 1894; E.B. et Cie 62). Piano part is reduction by Vincent d'Indy of orchestral score. No account has been taken of this score

E2 Second edition, E minor, vocal line in treble clef (E. Baudoux, 1894; E.B. et Cie 741). Piano part is Duparc's own.

E3 *Mélodies, nouvelle édition complète*, E minor, vocal line in treble clef (Rouart, Lerolle et Cie, 1911; A.R. 5740, L.& Cie)

E4 Revised orchestral score, E minor, vocal line in bass clef (Rouart, Lerolle et Cie, n.d.; dépôt légal, 1913; E.B. et Cie 69)

The first performance with piano was given at the 20th concert of the Société Nationale on 8 February 1873 by Marie Dufriche, accompanied by Vincent d'Indy. The first performance of the original orchestral score was given at the 70th concert of the Société Nationale on 13 May 1877; the singer was Numa Auguez, the conductor Edouard Colonne. The date of the first performance of the revised orchestral score is unknown.

Dedicated *à Monsieur Vincent d'Indy*

b1 (then on all odd-numbered bars up to and including b13)
    A1, **E4**: RH (2 bassoons, 2 horns), *f*; LH (violas, cellos), *p*

b2 (then on all even-numbered bars up to and including b12)
    A1, **E4**: orch, *crescendo* and *diminuendo* (on clarinets), climaxing on semiquaver 5; likewise (on violas and cellos), climaxing on semiquaver 9

b14   **E4**: orch (strings), *f*. RH, beat 3, demisemiquaver rest, followed by 7 demisemiquavers. All other sources: group of 7 demisemiquavers beginning on the beat

b15   **E4**: orch (cellos, basses), *sost.*

bb15, 16   **A1**, **E4**: bass line, these 2 bars phrased separately. **E1**: phrasing in b15 only. **A2**, **E2**: these bars phrased together

b17   **E4**: LH (violas, cellos, basses), *crescendo* from beat 3

b18   **E4**: LH (violas, cellos, basses), *crescendo* to beat 2; *diminuendo* to beat 3

b19   **E4**: vocal line, dim. from quaver 2; pf LH (violas, cellos, basses), *diminuendo* from beat 2

bb20, 22   **E4**: RH *ff*; LH *mf* (see b1 etc.)

b21   **A1**, **E4**: dynamics follow pattern of b2 etc. at higher level. Omitted from other sources, presumably in error. **E1**: *mf* throughout

b23   **A1**, **E1**, **E4**: vocal entry, *f*. Omitted from **A2**, **E2**, **E3**

b24   **E2**, **E4**: *plus large*. Omitted from **A2**, **E2**, **E3**, probably in error

b25   **A2**, **E2**, **E3**: LH, beat 3, ♮ missing before *a*. Present in **E4**

b32   **E4**: LH (bassoons, violas, cellos, basses), beat 1, *fp*; after beat 3, *dim.*

b33   **E4**: dynamics as in b1 etc. **A1**, LH, quaver 2, *f*♮. Omitted in **A2**, **E2**, **E3**

b34   **E4**: vocal line, beat 1, *poco a poco dim.* **A1**: LH (cellos, basses), beat 2, demisemiquaver 8, ♮ before *F*. Omitted in **A2**, **E2**, **E3**

b35   **E4**: RH (strings), *pp*; LH (bassoon, 2 horns), *mf*

b37   **E4**: RH (clarinets), *p*

b38   **E4**: orch (violins, violas), *ppp presque rien*

b41   **E4**: vocal line, *ff*

b42   **A1**, **E4**: vocal line, beat 3, duplet quavers. **A2**, **E2**, **E3**: crotchet plus triplet quaver

b43   **E4**: vocal line and orch (flutes, clarinets), ⌒ over minim

b46   **A2**, **E3**: vocal line, beats 2 and 3, upper alternative notes provided. **E4**: lower notes only

b47   **E4**: *doux et sombre*

b48   **E2**: LH, beat 1, rhythm double dotted in error; correct in b49

bb48, 49   **E4**: LH (flute), beat 1, appoggiatura *a″ b″* written as demisemiquavers at end of bb47 & 48

b50   **A1**, **E4**: LH (violas, cellos, basses), beat 1, *marcato*. Quaver & semiquaver rest. **A2**, **E2**, **E3**: dotted quaver. **E4**: LH, beat 3, final two quavers staccato

b61   **E4**: vocal line, *énergique et bien rythmé*

b63   **E4**: vocal line, *cresc.*

bb71, 72   Alternative notes present in all sources

b74   **A1**, **E2**, **E4**: vocal line, beat 3, crotchet & quaver. **E2**, **E3**: duplets (though not marked with 2)

bb74, 75, 77, 78
    A2, **E2**, **E3**: vocal line, *diminuendo*s on each beat. **A1**, **E4**: *diminuendo*s absent

bb82, 88   **E4**: LH (solo cello) *cantabile, crescendo*

bb82–84, 88–90
    In orchestral version (**E4**), arching line in bass from b82 (also b88) quaver 2 to b84 (also b90) beat 2 (an *f*♯) is played by solo cello, which also ties high *b*♮′ over bar line. Pianists wishing to observe this could take initial crotchet *b′* in RH

b94   **E2**, **E4**: LH (bassoon, trumpet, horn), beat 1 to beat 2, repeated *c′*, *mf*

b95   **E4**: orch (strings), beat 2, *crescendo*. **A1**, **A2**, **E2**: *crescendo* absent

bb95–96   **A1**, **E4**: vocal line, 'l'éternel fracas', every syllable accented. **A2**, **E2**: accents omitted

b96   **E4**: orch (clarinets, strings), beat 1, *diminuendo*. **E3**: beat 1 to beat 2, vocal line, tie from dotted crotchet to crotchet missing; present in all other sources. **E2**, **E4**: orch (bassoon, 2 horns), repeated *c*♯′, *f*

b98   **E4**: vocal line, beat 1, ⌒ mark, followed by *élargissez*; orch (flute, clarinet, cellos, basses) *élargissez, suivez*

b99   **A1**: originally 'a To' at b99, with *rit.* pencilled in on beat 2; then 'a To' at start of b100. **A2**, **E2**: these changes incorporated. **E3**: *poco rit.* **E4**: *rit.*

b100   **E2**: alternative bottom *E* absent

b106   **E4**: LH (timpani): *perdendo* on roll

No. 9: *La fuite*

Poem by Théophile Gautier, from *Poésies complètes* (Charpentier, 1858), p296

Sources

A Incomplete autograph MS, no dynamic indications, 3pp (pp1, 7, 8), unsigned, undated <d'Armagnac archives>

E First edition, E minor (E. Demets, 1903; E. 793 D.) Dedicated *à la mémoire d'Henri Regnault*

The first performance was given at the 20th concert of the Société Nationale on 8 February 1873 by Marie Wagner and Catherine Miquel-Chaudesaigues, accompanied by Vincent d'Indy

The surviving pages of **A** conform with **E**, with exception of b22, RH, quaver 3, where *a* is sharpened in anticipation of quaver 5

The following additions and changes to **E** have been made editorially:

b30   Vocal line, ♯ to *d"*s
bb44, 46, 48
          RH quaver 3 in each bar, **E**: *a*. Present edition prints *b*, by analogy with bb2, 4, 177 and 179
b82   Vocal line, quaver 3, ♭ to *e'''*
b85   Pf, *f*; RH, quaver 2, ♮ to *d'''*
b91   RH, quaver 3, ♭ to *b*
b100   RH, quaver 2, ♯ to *c"*
b101   RH, quaver 1, ♯'s to *c'''* and *g"*; LH, ♯ to *c'*
b103   RH, quaver 1, ♯ to *f"* correctly placed before *g"*
b107   RH, quaver 1, ♯'s to *c'''* and *g"*
bb112, 113
          RH, octava sign supplied, as in bb114–128.
b122   Vocal line, beat 2, ♮ to *f'*
b123   RH, quaver 1, ♮ to *f'''*, ♭ to *b"*
b129   Vocal line, ♮ to *f'*
b136   Vocal line, *f*
b139   Vocal line, ♭ to *b'*
b152   LH, beat 2, ♭ to *e'*
b161   RH, beat 2, ♭ to *e'* (absent also from **A**)
bb188–9   RH, phrase mark by analogy with succeeding passage

No. 10: *Elégie*

Prose translation by the composer's wife Ellie of the poem *Oh! Breathe not his name* from (Thomas) Moore's *Poetical Works Complete in one volume* (London, Longman, Brown, Green, Longman, and Roberts, 1857), p173

Sources

A Autograph MS, 5pp, signed near title and at end, undated; but dating from 1896 or after, since de Lassus died in that year. This MS was used for engraving of **E2** (see below)
<BnF Mus MS 1269>

E1 First version, F minor (supplement to *Journal de Musique*, ed. Armand Gouzien, II, no 85, 12 January 1878)

E2a First edition, F minor (E. Baudoux, 1901; E.B. et Cie 748)

E2b Transposition down to D minor for medium voice (E.B. et Cie 749)

E3 Supplement to *Le Monde musical*, 15 October 1908; 'Traduction en prose d'une poésie de Thomas MOORE sur la mort de Robert EMMET'. Transposition down to D minor

E4a *Mélodies, nouvelle édition complete*, F minor (Rouart, Lerolle et Cie, 1911; A.R. 5748bis L. & Cie)

E4b Transposition down to D minor for medium voice (A.R. 5749. L. & Cie)

It has not been possible to locate a second autograph MS, 4pp, signed, corresponding to **E2b**, given by Sacha Guitry to Adolphe Borchard

The first performance was given at the 61st concert of the Société Nationale on 30 December 1876 by Edmond Vergnet. At this concert Vergnet also gave the first performance of Franck's *Panis angelicus*, with Franck playing the organ.

E1: dedicated *à Monsieur E. Vergnet de l'Opéra*
A, **E2**, **E4**: dedicated *à la mémoire d'Henri de Lassus*
E3: no dedication
E1: *Andante*
b1   **A**, **E1**: *p*. In the absence of dynamic indications in later editions, this marking has been retained
bb3, 7   **E1**: RH, quavers 1–4, *e♮'*
bb8, 9   **E1**: vocal line, quavers 1–4, *diminuendo*
b10   **E1**: pf, quaver 1, *poco cresc*; no *diminuendo* in b11 in vocal line or pf
b14   **E1**: pf, quaver 1, *pp*
b15   **A**: vocal line, beat 1, *diminuendo*. Since this reading concurs with *diminuendo*s in two following bars, it has been adopted here
b18   **E2**, **E4**: vocal line, quaver 9, *c♮"*. **A**, **E1**, **E3**: *c♭"* (clearly correct)
bb24, 25 **E1**: no *crescendo* or *diminuendo*; pf, harmony simpler
b27   **E1**: *mais très peu* absent
b37   **E1**: *poco rit., A tempo* absent; vocal line, beat 3, *plus doux*; pf, beat 3, *dim.*
b38   **E1**: pf, beat 1, *più p*
b39   **E1**: vocal line, beat 1, *crescendo*
b40   **E1**: Duparc repeats harmony of bb5–14 exactly, beginning in b38; this necessitates repeat of words 'en secret répandues'. All later sources condense this passage by 2 bars, removing verbal repetition
bb40, 41 **E1**: vocal line, *cresc. molto*
bb43, 44 **E1**: vocal line different
b45   **E1**: pf, beat 1, *pp*; *dimin.* absent
b47   **E1**: *diminuendo* absent. **A**, **E1**, **E3**: beat 3, *riten./rit.*; **E2**, **E4**: no *riten.*
b48   **E1**: beat 1, 𝄂 no release marked

No. 11: *Extase*

Poem entitled *Nocturne* by Jean Lahor (Lemerre, 1875), p75. The repetition of the second line at the end of the song was made by Duparc

Sources

E1a First edition, D major (E. Baudoux, 1894; E.B. et Cie 63)

E1b Transposition down to B♭ major for medium voice (E.B. et Cie 741)

E2a *Mélodies, nouvelle édition complète* (Rouart, Lerolle et Cie, 1911; A.R. 5063. L & Cie)

E2b Transposition down to B♭ major for medium voice (A.R. 5741. L. & Cie)

E1 and **E2** are identical with the exception of b40, RH, where **E2** restores ♮'s to e″ and c″ dotted minims, omitted in error from **E1**. No autograph of this song has been located.

Dedicated *à Monsieur Camille Benoît*
The first performance was given at the 119th concert of the Société Nationale on 25 March 1882 by A. Leclère

No. 12: *Le manoir de Rosemonde*

Poem by Robert de Bonnières (1850–1915)

Sources

A1 Autograph MS, 3pp, D minor, unsigned, undated, pf part incomplete <d'Armagnac archives>

A2 Autograph MS, 3pp, D minor, signed, dedicated *à mon ami R. de Bonnières*, undated <d'Armagnac archives>

A3 Autograph MS, 4pp, C minor, signed on cover, undated, from collection of Charles Panzera <BnF Mus MS 20770>

E1a First edition, D minor (E. Baudoux, 1894; E.B. et Cie 65)

E2 Second edition, D minor (E. Baudoux, 1901; E.B. et Cie 743)

E2c Transposition down to B minor for medium voice (E.B. et Cie 745)

E3a *Mélodies, nouvelle édition complète*, D minor (Rouart, Lerolle et Cie, 1911; A.R. 5065. L. & Cie)

E3b Transposition down to B minor for medium voice (A.R. 5743. L. & Cie)

E4 Orchestral score, D minor (Rouart, Lerolle et Cie, n.d. [1913]; R.L. 9998. & Cie)

It was not possible to consult **A1** or **A2**. Remarks below are based on notes taken by Nancy van der Elst during her study of these sources.

The first performance was given at the 119th concert of the Société Nationale on 25 March 1882 by A. Leclère. The first performance of the orchestral version was given in the Montreux Kursaal on 17 October 1912; the singer was Jeanne Raunay, the conductor Ernest Ansermet.

E4: metronome mark, ♩.=92	
b9	**E4**: final ⌒ marked *court*
b14	**E2**: LH, beat 1, *crescendo* absent
b24	**E4**: orch (woodwind, trumpet, violas, cellos), beat 2, *cresc.*
b27	**E4**: orch (violins, violas), beat 2, *crescendo* to *ff*
bb27–29	**A1**, **A2**: these three bars originally four, with two different versions of harmonies in b27, LH figure of b29 brought forward to b28, and two bars given to unaccompanied declamation of altered vocal line for 'Si la course ne te harasse !'
b28	**A3**, **E2**: *riten.* absent
b29	**A3**, **E2**: LH, beat 1, *crescendo* absent
b36	**E2**: pf, *poco sfz* aligned with demisemiquaver. **E4**: *sfz* similarly placed, followed by *diminuendo*
b39	**E4**: orch (woodwind), beat 1, *diminuendo*
b39–40	b39, quaver 4 – b40, quaver 1. **A1**, **A2**, **A3**, **E4**: chords tied. **E1**, **E2**, **E3**: ties omitted in error
b40	**E4**: beat 1, no *crescendo*. All other sources: *crescendo*
b41	**E4**: orch (tutti), *cresc. molto*
b43	**E4**: RH, (flutes, horns, violins, cellos), beat 3, in unison with vocal line. All other sources: crotchet, 4-part G major chord
b44	**E4**: orch (woodwind, strings), *diminuendo* to *p*
b48	**E4**: LH (bassoon, cellos, basses), *crescendo*
b50	**E4**: LH (cellos, basses, timpani), staccato
b51	**E4**: RH, g♯ played by clarinet *poco sfz*
b53	**E2**: *pp* absent. **E4**: *un peu retenu* added to the *Ier Mouvt* found in all other sources
bb53, 54	**E4**: orch (strings) all notes staccato
b54	**E4**: orch (strings) rests correctly notated in 9/8; other sources in 3/4

No. 13: *Sérénade florentine*

Poem by Jean Lahor, from *L'Illusion* (Lemerre, 1875), p19

Sources

A1 Autograph MS, 2pp, D major, signed by composer and dated at end '7bre 1880'. From collection of composer's nephew, Monsieur Xavier Fouques Duparc <BnF Mus Cons MS 9852>

A2 Autograph MS, 2pp, F major, unsigned, undated. Pf part incomplete <d'Armagnac archives>

A3 Autograph MS, 2pp, F major, unsigned, undated <d'Armagnac archives>

E1a First edition, F major (E. Baudoux, 1894; E.B. et Cie 61)

E2 Second edition, F major (E. Baudoux,1901; E.B. et Cie, 739)

E3a *Mélodies, nouvelle édition complète*, F major (Rouart, Lerolle et Cie, 1911; A.R. 5061 L. & Cie)

E3b Transposition down to E♭ major for medium voice (A.R. 5739. L & Cie)

The first performance was given at the 119th concert of the Société Nationale on 25 March 1882 by A. Leclère

E: dedication, *à Monsieur Henry Cochin*
A1, **A2**, **E**: *Lento*. **A3**: *Pas vite*
A1, **A2**: RH, extra bar of triads before b1; all triads followed by quaver rest instead of tie

b2	**A1**: vocal line in bass clef
b6	**A1**, **A3**: quaver 6, *poco più f*. Followed in present edition
bb7, 8	**A1**, **A3**: LH, *decrescendo* through phrase. Followed in present edition
bb9, 10	**A1**: vocal line, *decrescendo* from b9, quaver 3 to b10, quaver 1; LH, from b9, quaver 6 to b10, quaver 4. Followed in present edition
b10	**A**: vocal line, slur joining dotted crotchets. Followed in present edition. **A**: LH, beat 2, dotted minim; **E**: dot omitted in error
b12	**A1**, **A2**: vocal line, beat 3, *dim.*

b17	**A1**, **A3**: LH, beat 1, *pp*. **A1**: 𝄞. released on beat 3
bb21–24	**A1**: RH, beat 1 of all bars, upper octave added to dotted minim
bb25–27	**A1**: RH, crotchet triads, without chromatic appoggiaturas
b26	**A1**, **A2**: vocal line, quaver 3, *dim*. **A1**: breath mark after 'alors'
b28	**A1**: pf, beat 3, single beat of quaver movement
bb28, 29	**A1**, **A3**: *poco allargando* to 'a t̲o̲' (*A tempo*) in b30; **A2**: to *A tempo* on b29, beat 2
b29	**A1**: RH, crotchet triads
b32	**A1**, **A2**: this bar absent
b33	**A1**: quaver 2, *perdendo*; *ppp* absent. **A2**, **A3**: no markings

No. 14: *Phidylé*

Poem by Charles-Marie-René Leconte de Lisle (1818–1894), from *Poèmes et poésies* (Marc Ducloux, 1855), p83. Of the ten stanzas, Duparc set Nos. 1, 2, 3 and 10

Sources

A1 Autograph MS, 12pp, A♭ major, unsigned, undated. In poor condition, with pf LH incomplete <d'Armagnac archives>

A2 Autograph MS, 1p, bb22–38, 56–58, A♭ major, unsigned, undated <d'Armagnac archives>

A3 Autograph MS of orchestral version, 20pp, A♭ major, signed at end, undated. This MS was used for engraving of printed score **E3** (see below) <Editions Salabert>

E1a First edition, A♭ major (E. Baudoux, 1894; E.B. et Cie 64)

E1b Transposition down to F♯ major for medium voice (E.B. et Cie 742)

E2a *Mélodies, nouvelle édition complète* (Rouart, Lerolle et Cie, 1911; A.R. et Cie 5530)

E2b Transposition down to F♯ major for medium voice (A.R. 5742. L. & Cie)

E3 Orchestral score (Rouart, Lerolle et Cie, 1909; A.R. 5068 & Cie)

It was not possible to consult **A1**. Remarks below are based on notes taken by Nancy van der Elst during her study of this source. **A3**, once held by Editions Salabert, cannot now be located. The first 4 bars are printed in *Cinquante ans de musique française*, ed. L. Rohozinski (Les Editions musicales de la Librairie de France, 1925), II, p21, with dedication *A Monsieur Ernest Chausson*; the title is spelt *Phydilé*. The last 5 bars are printed in Octave Séré, *Musiciens français d'aujourd'hui* (Mercure de France, 2/1921), p174, and in Sydney Northcote, *The Songs of Henri Duparc* (London, Dennis Dobson, 1949), opposite p106.

The first performance of *Phidylé* was given at the 188th concert of the Société Nationale on 5 January 1889 by Baudoin-Bugnet. Duparc worked on the orchestral version during the winter of 1892–3 and the first performance was given at the 232nd concert of the Société Nationale on 8 April 1893 by Eléanore Blanc. Although the programme indicates that the singer was Franz Warmbrodt, a letter from Duparc to Chausson speaks of wanting Mlle Blanc's address so that he can thank her and send her a copy of the song (*Revue musicale*, numéro spécial Ernest Chausson, December 1925, pp178–9). The conductor was Gabriel Marie. The concert also included premieres of Chausson's *Poème de l'amour et de la mer* (dedicated to Duparc) and Debussy's *La damoiselle élue*.

b3	**E3**: vocal line, beat 1, crotchet
b9	**E3**: vocal line, beat 4, *dim.* omitted
b11	**E3**: vocal line, *très doux* omitted
b19	**E3**: orch (flute, horn), *crescendo* through bar
b20	**E3**: RH (flute, horn), *expressif et soutenu*
b22	**E3**: *pp*. **A1**: this bar absent
b23	**A2**, **E3**: vocal line, initial minim rest; other sources, dotted minim
bb33, 34	**A1**: pf harmonies slightly different
b34	**A1**: LH, rising tenor line *f, g, a♭* absent. **E3**: pf, beat 1, *dim. subito* to end of bar; vocal line, beat 3, *dim.* omitted
b35	**E3**: orch, beat 2, *dim.* omitted
b36	**E3**: vocal line, *sempre* omitted
b37	**E3**: beat 2, *poco rall.* omitted
b38	**E3**: *A tempo* omitted
b43	**E3**: LH, quavers 6–8, *crescendo*
b44	**E3**: LH, beat 1, *p*
b45	**E3**: orch, beat 4, *dim.*
b47	**E3**: orch, beat 3, *pp*
b49	**E3**: orch (strings), beat 1, *p*; LH, tenor (solo cello) line marked *bien en dehors*
bb49–53	All editions place centre of hairpin after note 2 of line, although plainly unobtainable on pf. In bb74, 75, **A3** places hairpin much nearer to note 3 of (flute & horn) line, i.e. apex of phrase. Present edition follows this pattern in both passages
b56	**E3**: vocal line, *avec ampleur*; pf, quaver 2, *dim. subito*; quaver 3, *crescendo*
b57	**E3**: orch, beat 1 to beat 3, *diminuendo*
b58	**E3**: vocal line, *crescendo* omitted, but still present in orch
b59	**E3**: RH (violins), *cantabile*
b60	**E3**: vocal line, beat 4, *dim.* omitted
b62	**E3**: orch (strings), beat 1, *p*; RH, accent on (horn) *g♭'*
b65	**E3**: orch, beats 3,4, *diminuendo*
b66	**E3**: orch, beat 4, *cresc. molto*
b67	**E3**: vocal line, beat 3, *poco* omitted before *cresc.*
b68	**E3**: RH (violins), beat 1, *expressif*; beat 4, *b♭''*, *c'''* slurred
bb69–73	**E1**, **E2**: RH, one phrase per bar. **E3**: (violins) more articulated phrasing
b72	**E3**: alto (bassoon & cello) line, beat 1 to beat 3, *crescendo*; beat 3 to beat 4, *diminuendo*
b73	**E1**, **E3**: beat 3, *dim.*
b76	**E3**: beat 3, *rall.*
bb76, 77	**E1**: tie on *a♭* absent

No. 15: *Lamento*

Poem by Théophile Gautier, from *La Comédie de la Mort* (Dessessart, 1838), p305. Of the six stanzas, Duparc set Nos. 1, 3 and 6. Berlioz had previously set the entire poem under the title *Au cimetière*, as the fifth of the six songs in his *Nuits d'été*, published in 1841.

Sources

A Autograph MS, 3pp, D minor, signed at end, undated, bearing dedication *A mon cher maître & ami G. Fauré*. Over 'maître' Fauré has inscribed 'élève' (sic). Originally more complex, but slimmed down to produce version printed as **E1a** <d'Armagnac archives>

E1a First edition, D minor (E. Baudoux, 1894; E.B. et Cie 66)

E1b Transposition down to C minor for medium voice (E.B. 739)

E2 Second edition of **E1b** (E. Baudoux, 1901; E.B. et Cie 744)

E3a *Mélodies, nouvelle édition complète*, D minor (Rouart, Lerolle et Cie, 1911; R.L. 5066 & Cie)

E3b Transposition down to C minor for medium voice (A.R. 5744. L. & Cie)

The first performance was given at the 155th concert of the Société Nationale on 4 April 1885 by Madame Storm

E1a and **E3a** are identical, as are **E1b**, **E2** and **E3b**

E: dedication, *à Monsieur Gabriel Fauré*

bb3, 4	**A**: pf, beats 3 and 4, different harmonies; definitive version sketched above
b8	**A**: vocal line, beats 3 and 4, crotchet *a'*, quavers *bb'*, *c''*
b11	**A**: vocal line, breath mark after 'couchant'. Printed in this edition
bb14–17	**A**: pf, these bars crossed out; but four chords merely differently disposed (see below)
b15	**A**: vocal line, beats 1 and 2, phrase mark over *a'*, *d'*. Printed in this edition
b16	**A**: pf, beat 3, 1st inversion of G♭ major; vocal line, breath mark after "terre"
b17	**A**: pf, all three chords differently disposed
b19	**A**: vocal line, beats 2–4, minim *a'*, quavers *bb'*, *c''*
b21	**A**: vocal line, beat 2, breath mark after 'plaint'. Printed in this edition
b25	**A**: *un peu plus animé* crossed out
bb25, 26	**A**: pf, inner parts more complex; definitive version written at end of song
b34	**A**: RH, *crescendo* and *diminuendo* specifically applied to top part. This indication followed in present edition
b38	**A**: *riten.* on beat 3
b39	**A**: pf, beat 1, ***pp***
b39–40	**A**: RH, *d'* semibreve tied to minim. Printed as phrase mark in all published sources
bb39, 40	**A**: pf, figuration different; definitive version written on stave below; *poco a poco dim.* absent
b40	**A**: beat 3, *riten.*
b41	**A**: beat 1, ***ppp***; *1° tempo* crossed out

No. 16: *Testament*

Poem by Armand Silvestre (1837–1901), from *Les Ailes d'or* (Charpentier, 1880), p97

Sources

A Autograph MS, 6pp, C minor, unsigned, undated <d'Armagnac archives>

A2 Autograph MS of orchestral score, 22pp, C minor, signed, undated. This MS was used for engraving of published score (**E3**, see below) <Editions Salabert>

E1 First edition, C minor (E. Baudoux, 1894; E.B. et Cie 67)

E2 *Mélodies, nouvelle édition complète* (Rouart, Lerolle et Cie, 1911; A.R. 5067. L. et Cie)

E3 Orchestral score (Rouart, Lerolle et Cie, n.d. [1913]; R.L. 9994 & Cie)

It was not possible to consult **A1**. Remarks below are based on notes taken by Nancy van der Elst during her study of this source. Nor was it possible to consult **A2**, which cannot now be located.

The first performance was given at the 269th concert of the Société Nationale on 16 April 1898 by Lucien Berton. The first performance of an early orchestral version was given at the 292nd concert of the Société Nationale on 16 March 1901; the singer was again Lucien Berton, the conductor probably Vincent d'Indy. The first performance of the definitive orchestral version has not been traced with certainty, but may have been at the 'Festival Duparc' held in the Montreux Kursaal on 17 October 1912; the singer was Jeanne Raunay, the conductor Ernest Ansermet.

E: dedication, *à Madame Henri de Lassus (née Boissonnet)*
E3: metronome mark, ♩. = 69

b1	**E3**: quaver 9, *mf*
b3	**E3**: orch, quaver 1, *dim.*; quaver 9, ***p***. Vocal line, quaver 5, cautionary ♮ to *d'* added editorially
b5	**E1**, **E2**: vocal line, final quaver, *b♮'*; **E3**: *c♭* (see b50)
b7	**E1**, **E2**: vocal line, beat 1, quaver plus quaver rest; **E3**: quaver, followed by no rest. But on repeat of this phrase in b52, quaver is replaced by crotchet. Present edition follows latter reading in both bars. **E1**, **E2**: LH, semiquaver 15, *c♮'*; **E3** (violas): *c♭'*
b8	**E3**: RH, beat 1, *sfz* on *d''*; quaver 9, *dim.*
b10	**E1**, **E2**: vocal line, beat 3, quaver plus quaver rest; **E3**: crotchet. **E1**, **E2**: RH, phrasing over whole bar; **E3**: phrasing as printed here. **E1**, **E2**: LH, semiquaver 11, ♮ omitted before *b*; **E3** (clarinet): ♮ restored
b12	**E1**, **E2**: *cresc*; ***f***. **E3**: orch, beat 1, *cresc. molto*; RH, quaver 9, ***ff***
b21	**E1**, **E2**: vocal line, *decrescendo* on beat 3. **E3**: from beat 2, and in pf
b24	**E1**, **E2**: beat 1, *un peu plus animé*; vocal line, *mf*. **E3**: both indications omitted. LH (solo cello), beat 2 (beat 1, minim), *en dehors*
b27	**E1**, **E2**: vocal line, phrase mark discontinued; **E3**: carried over to beat 1
b28	**E1**, **E2**: after beat 2, *dim.* **E3**: *dim.* omitted
b29	**A1**: vocal line, beat 3, *appassionato*. **E3**: *passionné*
bb30, 31	**A1**: LH, triplet quaver rhythms
b33	**E1**, **E2**: vocal line, beat 2, *cresc.* **E3**: *cresc.* omitted
b35	**A1**: RH, central note, *b♮*. **E3**: vocal line, last quaver, ***ff*** *à pleine voix*
b36	**E1**, **E2**: beat 1, *A tempo*; beat 2, ***p***. **E3**: ⌢, ***pp*** on beat 1; *A tempo* on beat 2, ***p*** omitted
b37	**E1**, **E2**: LH, semiquaver 16, ♮ omitted before *A*; **E3** (cellos, basses, bassoon): ♮ restored
b38	**E1**, **E2**: vocal line, beat 1, *à pleine voix*. **E3**: ***ff***, *pressez un peu*
bb40–42	**E3**: vocal line, alternative lower option added
b43	**E3**: beat 2, ⌢ mark added; final quaver, *A tempo*, ***p*** *expressif*. **E1**, **E2**: *mf*
b44	**E3**: quaver 9, *mf en dehors*
b46	**E3**: *court* over ⌢. Beat 3, ***f***; **E1**, **E2**: *mf*
b48	**E3**: beat 1, *dim*; pf (flute, bassoon), quaver 9, *mf*

b50	**E3**: vocal line, quaver 9, c♭ (see b5)
b52	**E1**, **E2**: vocal line, beat 1, quaver plus quaver rest. **E3**: crotchet. **E1**, **E2**: LH, semiquaver 15, c♮′; **E3**: c′ (see note to b7)
b53	**E3**: beat 1, orch (cor anglais, horn, violins), *sfz*
b54	**E1**, **E2**: vocal line, beat 3, *più f*. **E3**: omitted
b55	**E1**, **E2**: vocal line, beat 3, quaver plus quaver rest. **E3**: crotchet. **E1**, **E2**: LH, semiquaver 11, ♮ omitted before b′; **E3** orch (clarinet): ♮ restored
b57	**E1**, **E2**: vocal line, beat 1, *f*. **E3**: omitted. **E1**, **E2**: pf, beat 1, *cresc.*; final quaver, *f*. **E3**: *cresc. molto*; *ff*
b59	**E3**: RH, quaver 9, *mf*
bb65–66	**E1**, **E2**: song ends on b66, beat one, as printed in present edition. **E3**: ends on b65, beat 3. On beat 2, sextuplets decelerate to quadruplets; on beat 3, there is a crotchet with a ⌒

No. 17: *La vie antérieure*

Poem by Charles Baudelaire, from *Les Fleurs du mal* (Michel Lévy, 1868), p103

Sources

A Autograph MS, 5pp, E♭ major, signed near title and at end, undated. This MS was used for engraving of **E1** (see below). From collection of Guy Ropartz <BnF Mus MS 15129>

E1a First edition, E♭ major (E. Baudoux, 1901; E.B. et Cie 752)

E1b Transposition down to C major for medium voice (E.B. et Cie 753)

E2a *Mélodies, nouvelle édition complète* (Rouart, Lerolle et Cie, 1911; R.L. 5752 & Cie)

E2b Transposition down to C major for medium voice (R.L. 5753 & Cie)

E3 Orchestral score (Rouart, Lerolle et Cie, s.d.[1913]; R.L. 9876 & Cie)

The first performance was given at a concert of the Groupe de XX in Brussels on 5 March 1903 by Elisabeth Delhez. The first performance of the orchestral version was given in the Montreux Kursaal on 17 October 1912; the singer was Jeanne Raunay and the conductor Ernest Ansermet.

E: Dedicated *à Monsieur J. Guy Ropartz*
E3: metronome mark, ♩=54

bb1–13	**E3**: b♭ trumpet octaves marked *bien rythmé*, with separation marks before final semiquavers (pf, RH)
b15	Duparc wrote to his editor, 23 April 1913: 'Pas de changement de mouvement dans *La vie antérieure* à la lettre B: un peu plus d'animation ne fait pas mal au piano, quoiqu'on presse toujours plus que je ne voudrais -; mais à l'orchestre, je préfère que le mouvement ne change pas : il est bien suffisamment dans l'accompagnement. D'ailleurs même dans la partition de piano, vous pourrez faire effacer l'indication quand on fera un nouveau tirage.' ('No change of speed in *La vie antérieure* at letter B [b15]: a little more animation doesn't do any harm in the piano version, even though people always hurry more than I would like-; but in the orchestral version I prefer the speed to remain constant: the effect is already there in the accompaniment. In fact, even in the piano version you can remove the indication when you reprint.') <Editions Salabert> Indication has remained in place until present edition **E3**: orch, *p*
b17	**E3**: RH, beat 3, g♭″; (woodwind) beats 2–4 phrased
b18	**E3**: RH (violins, violas), semiquavers 9, 10, cautionary ♮'s to d′, d″
b21	**E1**: no *accelerando* until b29. **E2**: *augmentez et pressez toujours*, up to *A tempo* in b32. **E3**: LH (cellos, double basses, 4th horn), *sfz* on beat; *pressez peu à peu* delayed until b29
b24	**E3**: *Ier Mouvement* refers to *A tempo* at end of b32. **E1**: no indication of tempo change
b28	**A**, **E1**, **E2**: vocal line, *ff*. **E3**: *f*
b29	**E3**: *pressez un peu*
b32	**A**, **E3**: pf, orch, beat 3, *sffz sec*
bb32, 33	**A**, **E1**, **E2**: b32, beat 4, *largement et à pleine voix*; b33, beat 1, *Ier Mouvement*. **E3**: b32, beat 4, *A tempo, à pleine voix*
b33	**A**, **E1**, **E2**: pf, *pp*; **E3** (strings), *ppp*. **A**, **E1**, **E2**: vocal line, breathing mark. **E3**: omitted
bb41, 42	**A**, **E1**, **E2**: pf, LH then RH, *marcato*. **E3**: *cantabile*. Both indications retained here. **A**, **E1**, **E2**: no comma after 'nus'; **E3**: comma retained, following Baudelaire. It is suggested that singers make only the smallest hiatus here, so as not to disturb the visionary atmosphere
b45	**A**, **E1**, **E2**: *poco rall.* **E3**: delayed until b46, beat 2
b48	**E1**, **E2**: pf, phrase mark finishes at end of bar; **E3**: orch (cor anglais) continues to b51, beat 1
b50	**A**, **E3**: RH, beat 3, c♭. **E1**, **E2**: c♮
bb51–55	**A**, **E1**, **E2**: RH, single phrase from b51, beat 3 to b56, beat 3. **E3**: orch (cor anglais) melody divided into two phrases
b55	**A**, **E1**: semibreve octave A♭. **E2**: LH, as printed. **E3**: LH (cellos, basses), beat 1, *crescendo* up to A♭, then *diminuendo*; rendered here by stress marking. RH chords remain *pp*
b56	**A**, **E1**, **E2**: beat 3, *un peu ralenti*. **E3**: beat 1, *un peu retenu jusqu'à la fin*
b58	**A**: RH, final quaver, a♭, *f* tied across barline. **E1**, **E2**: ties omitted. **E3**: dissonance resolves on to E♭ minor on beat 1 of b59. Present edition follows **A**

The Art of French Song
Edited by Roger Nichols

VOLUME 1

Niedermeyer	Le lac
Berlioz	Absence
Gounod	Ô ma belle rebelle
Viardot	Fleur desséchée
Franck	S'il est un charmont gazon
Massé	Consolation
Lalo	Ballade à la lune
Saint-Saëns	La sérénité
Delibes	Chanson espagnole
Bizet	Pastorale
Massenet	Nuit d'Espagne
Chabrier	L'île heureuse
Paladilhe	Sérénité de la nuit
Fauré	Lydia
Fauré	Après un rêve
Duparc	Extase
Chausson	Le colibri
Debussy	Mandoline
Debussy	C'est l'extase langoureuse
Satie	Daphénéo
Satie	Spleen
Séverac	Ma poupée chérie
Dupont	Chanson des noisettes
Poulenc	La Grenouillère

VOLUME 2

Reber	Guitare
Gounod	Le soir
Gounod	Premier jour de mai
Viardot	Les deux roses
Viardot	La mésange
Franck	Nocturne
Massé	Souvenirs
Lalo	Chant breton
Saint-Saëns	Chanson triste
Bizet	Vieille chanson
Massenet	Madrigal
Massenet	Ouvre tes yeux bleus
Chabrier	Les cigales
Paladilhe	Sonnet de Pétrarque
Fauré	Automne
Fauré	Le secret
Duparc	La vie antérieure
Chausson	Nocturne
Debussy	Le jet d'eau
Satie	Sylvie
Séverac	Philis
Honneger	Automne
Poulenc	Fleurs

'... these books are indispensible to anyone with the same sense of delight and adventure that characterizes this wonderful repertoire – one of France's unsung, or at least under-sung, national treasures.'
Graham Johnson

LONDON • FRANKFURT/M • LEIPZIG • NEW YORK
www.editionpeters.com

30 Italian Songs and Arias

of the seventeenth and eighteenth centuries

Selected and edited by Roger Nichols

 including CD of accompaniments

Italian songs and arias of the 17th and 18th centuries have for many years been essential repertoire for anyone learning to sing. But this music is principally known in romantic adaptations which the original composers would barely recognize. This new collection of 30 songs and arias (based on the "standard 24", together with other pieces typical of the Italian style) recreates the clearer and cleaner – and easier to play – accompaniment style of the 17th and 18th centuries. In addition to authentic editions of the music, the book contains invaluable information which will help singers interpret and perform this repertoire:

- word-by-word translations (Italian–English) of the original text
- English singing translations
- IPA transliterations of the Italian text
- historical notes about each song

A CD, containing recordings of the piano accompaniments, is included with the book.

EP7743a: medium-high voice
EP7743b: medium-low voice

I am delighted to see Parisotti's ubiquitous anthology recast with such learned courtesy. Roger Nichols has shed all outdated features, adding instead invaluable information and suggestions; this choice of pieces celebrates even better the genius of Italian baroque song, and I hope to see it used everywhere!

Emma Kirkby

CONTENTS

Giulio Caccini: *Amarilli, mia bella*

Claudio Monteverdi: *Lasciatemi morire*

Marco da Gagliano: *Valli profonde*

Sigismondo d'India: *Torna il sereno Zefiro*

Giacomo Carissimi: *Vittoria, mio core*; *Crudo amore*

Barbara Strozzi: *L'amante bugiardo*; *La vendetta*

Giovanni Legrenzi: *Che fiero costume*

Giuseppe Torelli: *Tu lo sai*

Alessandro Scarlatti: *Già il sole dal Gange*; *O cessate di piagarmi*; *Sento nel core*; *Le violette*; *Se Florinda è fedele*

Antonio Lotti: *Pur dicesti, bocca bella*; *Padre, addio*

Giovanni Bononcini: *Non posso disperar*; *Per la gloria d'adorarvi*

Antonio Caldara: *Sebben, crudele*; *Alma del core*; *Come raggio di sol*

Francesco Durante: *Vergin, tutt'amor*; *Danza, danza, fanciulla*

Francesco Conti: *Quella fiamma*

Anonymous: *Nina*

Christoph Willibald von Gluck: *O del mio dolce ardor*

Tommaso Giordani: *Caro mio ben*

Giovanni Paisiello: *Nel cor più non mi sento*

Alessandro Parisotti: *Se tu m'ami*

LONDON • FRANKFURT/M • LEIPZIG • NEW YORK
www.editionpeters.com